I0040985

Marketing Essentials for Independent Lodgings

Marketing Essentials for Independent Lodgings

Pamela Lanier and Marie Lanier

BEP BUSINESS EXPERT PRESS

Marketing Essentials for Independent Lodgings

Copyright © Business Expert Press, LLC, 2017.

All rights reserved. No part of this publication may be reproduced, stored in a retrieval system, or transmitted in any form or by any means—electronic, mechanical, photocopy, recording, or any other except for brief quotations, not to exceed 400 words, without the prior permission of the publisher.

First published in 2017 by
Business Expert Press, LLC
222 East 46th Street, New York, NY 10017
www.businessexpertpress.com

ISBN-13: 978-1-63157-596-9 (paperback)
ISBN-13: 978-1-63157-597-6 (e-book)

Business Expert Press Tourism and Hospitality Management Collection

Cover and interior design by Exeter Premedia Services Private Ltd., Chennai, India

First edition: 2017

10 9 8 7 6 5 4 3 2 1

Printed in the United States of America.

Thank you to all the bed & breakfasts, inns, boutique hotels, and ecolodges who have been so generous over the years with both their hospitality and their knowledge. Without you, and every property like you, this book would not have happened. Continue doing what you do, brightening the world one morning at a time.

And welcome to our world, Zena Renee Reimann Valdes!

Abstract

Marketing a small, independently owned lodging business can be difficult. Marketing Essentials for Independent Lodgings outlines how to get a business's name out there, attract consumers, and navigate the dicey world of social media and an online presence. Descriptions of traveler demographics, how to get the word out about a property, and how to make a property unique are all talked about at depth. The goal of this book is to help small lodgings flourish, and it does so by including lists of actions that can be taken this week, this month, or this year to help positively impact the bottom line. Also included is a specific marketing outline that can be adapted to an individual business, giving business owners a timeline and plan they can follow.

Keywords

marketing, bed & breakfast, boutique hotel, ecotourism, guesthouse, inn, lodge, lodging, OTA, print marketing, public relations, social media, travel agent

Contents

Special Thanks

We extend special thanks to those who worked on this project, without them this book would not have happened.

Jessica Hughes, who served as senior editor and coordinator, and
Inci Haksoz, who generously shared her knowledge with us

IUCN's Commission on Education and Communication

And the Business Expert Press team, which included:
Scott Isenberg
Professor Betsy Stringam and
Exeter team, India

Acknowledgments

Many of the chapters came in full or in part from professionals and industry leaders. We would like to thank them by name here. To read more about them, refer to the Author Biographies in the back of the book.

Thank you to:

Steve Pinetti
Patricia McCauley
Lisa Kolb
Julia Guerra
Carolin Lusby
Kris Ullmer
Marci Bracco Cain
Heather Turner
Erika Richter and all who contributed from the American Society of Travel Agents

Introduction

No matter how big or small, every lodging property needs to have a strategic business plan, and the heart of that plan should be the culture behind the property goals.

The owner, through their words and actions, creates this culture which becomes the purpose or the "why" which is tactically embodied in how the staff delivers the desired guest experience.

The overarching goal should be that every guest will want to make a return visit and to share their terrific experience with their friends and peers. This isn't new news, but sometimes in a 24/7 business, owners and staff can lose sight of this vital focus.

A staff that responds from their hearts and granted autonomy that allows them to follow their instincts, create the necessary foundation for the kind of personalized experience today's traveler is going out of their way to find.

All you need to do is look at all the consumer sites. People talk about great places they have visited but most of all they highlight specific employees, share how well they were cared for and how they were made to feel.

Pamela has done a terrific job in highlighting the critical essentials for an overall marketing strategy for independently owned lodgings. I would like to highlight Word of Mouth as the most powerful of all sales marketing tools, especially today with the greater need for transparency and with all the social and digital resources now at hand.

It's so important for you, the operator to share "share-worthy" images via social channels that potentially prompt your guests to review your property on third-party sites like Trip Adviser and Yelp.

Additionally, a manager on staff should respond to social posts, but even better if it's you, the owner. Don't leave people hanging. If you create a Facebook page, social media account, or some such, people expect you to respond to their comments, both good and bad. Doing so shows that you care about the guest experience and that you're actively listening. Consumers expect businesses to listen these days.

LISTEN, LISTEN, LISTEN. Designate a hash tag for your property, and follow along with that hash tag on Instagram and Twitter. When people click on your hash tag, you want them to see a steady stream of real guest photos. We know this provides the layer of authenticity that will push potential guests over the edge to actually book.

It takes effort and time to manage your social strategy but again it's critical for your success to engage with travelers. Always thank them for posting. It's also a great way to stay fresh in their minds, so that they're more likely to recommend you after their trip.

These days, travelers (especially leisure) care less about what you have to say about your property and more about what real guests have to say about the experience you provided them.

—by Steve Pinetti

A Word from the Author

"Hospitality: It's more than just a smile"

—Jim Kuhns

This quote from veteran industry consultant and longtime American Express VP perfectly describes the necessity of addressing hospitality first when discussing this industry, even in a book focused on marketing. And it's really simple why. Everything that one does in providing a cozy place to stay, delicious food, and a comfortable atmosphere hinges upon the success of conveying to one's guests the spirit of welcome, open-mindedness, and the desire to help, which are of the essence in this endeavor.

In Steve Pinetti's introduction, he expresses this concept well, having learned it from Bill Kimpton a hotelier noted for his business smarts, real-estate genius, and low-key charisma. The first thing Bill expressed to me when I first met him was that his mission was hospitality. Not his business credo. Not his bottom line. Not even his mission statement. It was his personal heartfelt mission to provide a special brand of hospitality to a diverse and inclusive clientele that illuminated all aspects of Kimpton Hotels as it developed. From human resource policies, groundbreaking and ever expanding green practices, and their unparalleled success in promoting their hotels in ways that have more to do with creativity than traditional big budget marketing.

To give a little background, as a communications major in college, I was very fortunate to have the opportunity to work closely with the innovative Marshall McLuhan who coined the phrase and was the first to really internalize the message "the medium is the message." Starting from that premise I synthesized what I learned both in college and in my younger years working in a family business into a marketing-based communications concept. I'd had the privilege of traveling with my parents for one month every year, and both my folks knew how to appreciate, utilize, and enjoy the facilities and services of small independently owned lodging.

A post-college trip to Europe introduced me to European style pensiones, B&Bs and zimmer frei, and as a young woman traveling alone, I quickly realized I would be safer in a hosted environment, where my gracious hosts could direct me on where (and where not) to go. My hosts—almost without exception—were genuinely interested in sharing their culture, cuisine, and family celebrations with me, and I had a truly remarkable and life-changing trip. At that time—pre-internet— guidebooks reigned as the way for travelers to find like minds and somewhat tried and true accommodations. Train stations had kiosks with booklets describing local accommodations, usually through Rick Steves' guidebooks or the Let's Go series, and as a solo, independent traveler, I appreciated having these places pre-vetted for me.

When I returned to the United States, I looked for similar guidebooks and came up with a very limited, highly regional and idiosyncratic selection. Yet, in taking road trips around northern CA, I was seeing signs popping up for Bed & Breakfasts all over. Even in the weekend Sunday paper, Richard Paoli, a like-minded independent traveler and the editor of SF Examiner's travel section, regularly wrote about the exciting new phenomenon popping up around the Bay Area and in East Coast resort enclaves such as Bucks County, Pennsylvania and Woodstock Vermont, and a small sprinkling almost everywhere else. I had the good fortune to know a publisher and rather out of the blue I proposed a European-style independent lodging guidebook to them. This was John Muir Press, internationally renowned for teaching "idiots" how to repair their Volkswagen and a couple of travel books such as the iconic *People's Guide to Mexico*. To my utter shock, while I was walking down the beach from dinner one night, near Manzanillo, Mexico, John and Eve Muir said "We like this idea, go get started. When can you have it ready?" I quickly agreed, claiming research was underway (a file folder with 10 of Richard and other's news clippings) and I, with a great deal of help from the sensational librarians at the Oakland Business library, began a massive data-gathering endeavor. Much to our amazement, after about 3 months, we had a list of over 2,000 independent properties. My initial proposal only called for a few hundred, so we decided to compile a database. My librarian friends insisted, "No file cards," so from the very beginning, the foundations of the book were properly digitized.

Much to our amazement, of the over 2,000 properties we found, around 1,200 innkeepers took the time to answer our questions, fill out the form, stamp it, and send it back to us. So the first editions of *The Complete Guide to Bed & Breakfasts, Inns and Guesthouses* featured over 1,200 properties. Now a directory, when it was released in 1983, it was among the first fully digital publishing projects in the United States. Since then, there have been 28 fully revised editions, with over 8,500 B&Bs, inns, and guesthouses joining its pages. Four years later, we also published a coffee table style directory, with an entire page devoted to each property, named *Elegant Small Hotels: Boutique and Luxury Accommodations* to serve the growing trend toward boutique hotels, a larger but still personally designed hospitality. Elegant Small Hotels is now in its 25 anniversary edition.

Right from the first edition, the B&B guidebook took off and we could tell that we had tapped into a growing demand from Americans, many of whom had traveled abroad, to move beyond the often sterile experiences of motels and large-scale chain hotels and experience a more immersive, individualized form of hospitality.

Many people want that now, more than ever, which is why hospitality has to come first in any business consideration of the small lodging market.

Included in this book are ideas I've been fortunate enough to harvest from thousands of innkeepers and hoteliers, some of which we have developed together as time has passed and technology has developed. I've made presentations at over 100 of statewide or regional tourism stakeholders' conferences over the years, but it's the feedback from the audience, that helps me discover the best marketing practices for the real-life independent innkeeper.

—Pamela Lanier

PART I

Marketing and Pricing Basics

Location, Print, Community Outreach, Groups, and More

CHAPTER 1

First Impressions: Hospitality

What do travelers really want from a lodge, property, or inn? This is one of the most frequently asked questions at lodging association meetings and new inn seminars. My personal experience, combined with the experiences shared by inngoers in the letters and e-mails we have received indicate conclusively *that the single most important attribute of an inn are its innkeepers*. You are the ones who make the difference at your inn by creating a unique ambiance, welcoming your guests warmly and providing them with your own special brand of hospitality.

The word "hospitality" first appeared in the English language in the 14th century, and hospitable as an adjective first appeared circa 1570. It is defined as:

1. Giving to generous and cordial reception of guests
2. Promising or suggesting generous and cordial welcome
3. Offering a pleasant or sustaining environment
4. Kindness in welcoming guests or strangers

Studies on the Bed & Breakfast industry repeatedly conclude that the elements that contribute to guest satisfaction are service oriented. Small inns have a distinct advantage in this area because guests increased opportunities to interact with the innkeepers mean they develop very personal impressions. These impressions leave with your guests, exponentially increasing guest numbers when the word-of-mouth is excellent.

Recent surveys on guest satisfaction indicate that many of the top 10 qualities yielding the highest ratings are service oriented. Small inns have a distinct advantage in their ability to provide customer service because the increased opportunities for guests and innkeepers to interact. These impressions can have significant impact on your word-of-mouth marketing, which, if it is good, can ultimately lead to increased reservations. It is understood in this survey that minimum inn standards (including impeccable cleanliness, good lighting the property, and safety throughout considerations) are already in place. Five inn qualities that produce guest satisfaction, ranked in order of importance, are as follows:

1. Good value for the price (whatever that price point may be)
2. Overall privacy and peaceful atmosphere
3. Innkeeper's ability to make guests feel comfortable
4. Attractive, comfortable atmosphere with appropriate amenities
5. Great food!

During my inn visits, I enjoy late afternoons when I can lounge in the public rooms, talk with fellow guests and the innkeeper about local attractions and other, lesser known, fun things to do, and great nearby hikes. If the innkeeper keeps a welcome guide and includes suggested activities and dining recommendations, it is usually the first thing I consult after checking in, as it makes my stay even more special. Quiet is important to me. I always know I will sleep soundly when I see an air filter or white-sound machine near the bed or hear the reassuring hum of the heating or air-conditioning system.

Waking up to a wonderful breakfast matters a lot. A good morning meal is sure to generate great conversations among the inn goers at the breakfast table. When possible, a multicourse breakfast can add an extra perk to a visitors stay Likewise, a breakfast with a set entree and numerous sideboard options, from cereals to fruits and breads, is just as satisfying. Guests are often counting on their breakfast to carry them through the better part of a day of sightseeing.

Innkeeping is a fabulous, multidimensional profession, but that's easy to forget amidst the hustle and bustle of this "total immersion" lifestyle. It's important to remember that beyond the personal gratification that innkeeping affords, the very act of providing hospitality is a wonderful gift to offer others. Hospitality is a cherished tradition throughout cultures worldwide and is perhaps summed up by one of my favorite quotes: "Don't forget to entertain strangers, for by doing so some have unknowingly entertained angels."

Further reading

The Heart of Hospitality by Micah Solomon

CHAPTER 2

Total Media Marketing

In order to make a successful business out of lodging, you must continuously and creatively market your property on many different levels. You want to let as many potential guests know about your place as possible, and since people search out information in many different ways, it's important to utilize all media that is available.

Total Media Marketing: This sounds technical, but what it means is *using all the resources at your disposal* to get your name out to the public.

There are many ways to go about promoting your property. This chapter covers print, radio and TV, promotions, food and drink, business and commercial, community service and outreach, and of course, the core of what you do, people.

Many of the following ideas can be used as a springboard for other actions.

Print

Guidebooks: They are among the top three sources for reservations, especially for mature and affluent guests. Don't overlook this source for guests and advertise if necessary.

Magazines, chamber of commerce guides, regional tourist publications: Visit your Chamber of Commerce and bring something personal (like your signature cookies) and some brochures. Share your inn's story in publications. Tourist magazines submit local history articles. Participate in their after-hours membership mixers and offer to hold one at your location.

Local newspapers: Get to know the lifestyle and travel editors and invite them to breakfast. Smaller papers use fillers, so send them an article photos. It may take time, but they will most likely use it. Issue press releases well in advance, when special events are planned. Find out when they have an annual Visitor's Guide and get included. Donate a free room mid-week to a cause the paper is sponsoring. You'll see your inn in print over and over.

Travel writers: Contact the International Food and Wine Travel Writers Association at http://ifwtwa.org/ and the Society of American Travel Writers at www.satw.org. Tell them what is outstanding about your inn and the personal touches you offer. Invite them for a visit over breakfast, lunch, or tea, to talk. Invite *bona fide* writers for a complimentary mid-week night stay.

Public relation firms: They can help you develop your brochure, and provide you with quality photographs of your property. They can assist you in making up a Press Kit, and their contacts could help you to receive magazine exposure.

Brochures: Reciprocate with other local businesses display their brochures in exchange for them displaying yours. Talk to restaurants, health clubs, delis, tourist attractions, and museums. Get the word out!

Recipes: Send your recipes anywhere and everywhere they might be printed, including Internet sites. Create a small recipe booklet. Make laminated bookmarks to give away, with a prime recipe on one side and your inn information on the other side.

Postcards: Leave a postcard with a professional quality photo of your place in each guestroom with a postage stamp and pen, allowing guests to send a quick note to friends. It is a nice guest perk and connects you to potential guests you might never have reached. The personal touch of a piece of actual mail makes an impression.

Radio and TV

Sponsor weekly ads for weather, news or traffic reports. These are relatively inexpensive and will keep your name out there.

Donate a room mid-week to a cause or an event that the radio or your local public TV station is sponsoring. While they are promoting the event, you will hear your property's name mentioned numerous times.

Create a venue. Make your inn available for a reception or a fundraiser. Each time the fundraiser is promoted, your local inn's name will be mentioned.

Radio and TV stations will often work with you on a trade basis. In exchange for providing a room, you can get airtime of equal value. Then use a stay at your property to provide gifts to key clients or for prizes in contests.

Local talk shows or morning shows. Tell your inn's story on a local TV or radio station.

Promotions

Frequent-stayer. Have a program with discounts for return guests.

Monthly specials list. What does this consist of? It's simply your inn's monthly offerings of seasonal and timely special offers and packages. Make sure that each monthly entry is easy to flesh out with specifics and work them around local events. Send your specials to all the venues you can think of and include those specials in any newsletters or flyers you send out.

Theme a month. Have a Valentine's month—instead of a weekend in February. (Every guestroom displays a white box tied in red ribbon, containing some little chocolates, shortbread, or candies.) Try cooking weekends, a murder mystery event, wine-making weekends—tap into your creativity!

Ladies events. Most likely you have a high school, a college, a nursing school, or a beautician's college nearby promote an event for a sorority reunion, a girls' Super Bowl party, bachelorette party, spa day, and so on.

Offer a membership with lower prices for member stays or "bring a guest" events.

Food and Beverages

(Check your zoning laws to make sure you have the proper zoning and licenses.)

Local tastings. Team up with wineries for wine tastings to be held at the inn. Olive oil tastings and artisanal beer have also been growing in popularity, try getting in touch with local producers, breweries, and wineries and see if any would be willing to work with you to put together an event.

Local chefs. Might they offer a cooking class and dinner on a Saturday or Sunday night? You can package this with a weekend stay.

Workshops. Offer food and menu design classes.

Network. Plan an "hors d'oeuvres reception," and invite local businesses to meet the innkeepers and visit the inn over wine and cheese.

Signature dishes. Create a dish with a catchy name and serve it often. Word will spread, and friends of guests will want to try your dish firsthand.

Business and Commercial

Business travelers. Offer business rates, early breakfast, and free high-speed Wi-Fi. Business travelers will almost always bring their own laptop or tablet, but make sure you have a working printer and no dead zones. Consider preparing breakfast bags to-go so they can eat on the move.

Destination marketing. Get the uplift from government spending on state, county, and local tourism and visitors' centers. Destination Marketing is one of the key trends on the Internet. Make sure your property is well and correctly represented in these important state and federal venues, both print and digital.

Airline employees. They have an industry magazine, and you can also post your brochures in their break rooms. American Flight Attendants Union website is www.afacwa.org/.

Real-estate agents. Contact real-estate agents, their relocating clients may need a place to stay.

Hotel concierge. Get to know hotel concierges. When they are over-booked, they could have your card or brochures to hand out.

Convention and visitor's bureau. Check in with your convention bureau or mayor's office and get some up-to-the-moment information on conferences—large and small—coming to your area, including delegations of government employees, and so on. Contact local auditoriums and conference centers to see if they have any events booked that might bring out-of-town visitors. Send your lodging information to the sponsoring organizations, service clubs, churches, schools, and colleges, asking if they still need hotel rooms for the conference. Vendors, speakers, and VIPs may also need lodging. Remember, filling those weekday rooms is key to increasing your overall revenue.

Service clubs. Such as Rotary Club, Lion's Club, Women's Club of America, Sister Cities, and many others are established and reliable places to develop relationships with other business people and those who are active in the community.

Tour operators. Tour operators like all-inclusive packages, which include special offers, rental cars, and meals. You can work deals out with shuttle companies, restaurants, and rental car companies. You could cooperate with other inns to entice larger groups, and then refer your group to a special interest tour operator.

Weddings. Market yourself to wedding and event coordinators, and form an alliance with florists and catering companies who are likely to get that business.

Community Service

Sponsor or cosponsor a small event: This could be a car or a bicycle rally, a charity dinner or an auction, a girl's tea party, garden tours and garden club parties. Any of these will display your inn as a sponsor for the event.

Charity: Assist this charity throughout the year. Donate a small percentage of your room rate. Don't forget to advertise your good work in the pamphlets, check-in section, and of course, on your website.

Conferences: There are writing workshops for literary societies, teachers groups, and school board conferences that could be hosted by your inn.

Preservation and historic societies: These societies meet to have lunch and discussions. If you have a historical property, you could play host and share information about the rich history of your property.

Fundraisers: Feature or donate your inn for a fundraiser tour of homes. Offer free of charge stays to schools, and so forth, for fundraisers and other worthwhile causes and get thousands of dollars in free advertising whenever the fundraiser is mentioned.

Clubs: Contact local chapters of Moose, Lions, Rotary, Kiwanis, and Veterans of Foreign Wars. Contact interest clubs: gardening clubs, alumni organizations, fraternal orders, family-owned businesses, journaling workshops, sports car clubs, pharmaceutical reps., chess clubs, and knitting clubs, art guilds, motorcycle, car, gun or hunting clubs, bridge, and chess clubs. For every interest, there's a club somewhere, and many have annual events that bring people in from out of town.

Local businesses: Outside experts, interns, and trainees may need lodging. Offer a location for a staff meeting, a training session or a social event outside the office.

Civil servants: The Society of Government Meeting Professionals is geared to people who plan government meetings and those who supply services to government planners. Remember, traveling government employees get lodging allowances. Per Diem rates vary state to state and even between counties. See more information at http://www.sgmp.org/.

Military personnel: They are promoted and transferred to other bases throughout the world and often need interim housing. In addition, personnel come to the area for meetings, official business, and leisure activities. If you maintain contact with various squadrons and divisions at the local military base, you will find out who is in charge of outside sleeping rooms for overflow accommodations. The contracting office may have outside companies performing special duties and these people may require lodging. Armed Forces Vacation Club website: www. afvclub.com. Other departments to contact are: Scheduled Airline Travel Office (SATO), Information, Tickets and Tours (IT) office. If there is a Non-Commissioned Officers or an Officer's Wives Club, you could make a presentation at one of their meetings.

Universities: If your inn is near a university look at the student calendar and contact department heads for events that bring people into town. Contact deans' secretaries when dignitaries and speakers come to town, they can stay with you. Homecoming can bring many alumni to town, and most of them will need a place to stay!

Churches: Contact the clergy, assistant clergy or administrative specialists at the churches in your town. Many have special conferences for men, women, singles, couples, and seniors and may require extra housing. Their national speakers may draw extra people to your town. You could offer a percentage of the room rent as a tithe to the church.

Hospitals: You can provide stays for families of accident victims. Also, government accountants come to hospitals yearly and need a place to stay during their visit.

Funeral Directors: They could offer referrals to their clients who are hosting out-of-town relatives.

The Human Element

"Never underestimate Word of Mouth."

Your best resource is your enthusiastic guests. To ensure that each visitor positively reviews the accommodation and their experience, formal training should be provided to all staff at the accommodation. Every staff member should have an accurate information base that includes an understanding of the grounds and nearby areas, local attractions, information about the history of the property, and a general knowledge about the natural and cultural environment of the local area. Additionally, every employee should possess basic skills such as listening, problem solving, providing directions, and general customer service.

Finally, staff members should recognize that it is the extras that make a difference and keep visitors returning. Understanding that the customer is always right (even when they aren't) and treating guests with friendliness and respect, and having an admiration for the area go a long way. It is special attention to details such as this that makes visitors feel a unique connection to the area that they visit and encourages them to share their experiences with friends, family, and the online community. Consider having a referral discount for new guests and free stay or a free robe (with the hotel's logo, of course) for previous guests who refer three or five new visitors.

Cooperation

The spirit of "coopetition" (this simply means cooperating with competitors to everyone's benefit) especially among smaller business is the modality for the new millennium. Make sure that you are in this powerful mode. Contact your fellow innkeepers and hoteliers and see what you can do to help each other with mutual referrals when overbooking occurs or if a guest just wants something different. Additionally, contact the concierge staff at several of the better hotels in metro areas near you. Many of these professionals are the first ones to hear from a guest, perhaps in town for a conference, that they'd like to extend their stay. Developing a rapport can materially improve your occupancy rate.

Make sure you have a mechanism in place to send your excess bookings to one or more of you neighboring inns and vice versa.

Takeaways

- Think hard and discuss with others in your area, especially other travel-oriented businesses, and determine what is driving tourism in your area. Where are travelers coming from?

- Reach out to other businesses and consider joining organizations such as the chamber of commerce, service clubs, and more that will bring you in touch with other business people in your community. Always carry your business cards and hand them out freely. Join and circulate your community.
- Check in and update your listings with local reference books, online directories, state tourism sites, yellowpages, and so on and make sure that your information stays current. Entering your property name in one or several search engines may reveal listings you are unaware of. Are the results accurate?

CHAPTER 3

Marketing Your Passions

According to the U.S. Travel Association:

1. Nearly four out of five domestic trips taken are for leisure purposes (79 percent).
2. Top leisure travel activities for U.S. domestic travelers: (1) visiting relatives; (2) shopping; (3) visiting friends; (4) fine dining; and (5) beaches.
3. Overseas arrivals represent 49.5 percent of all international arrivals, yet account for 80.5 percent of total international travel spending.
4. Each overseas traveler spends approximately $4,400 when they visit the United States and stays for an average of 18 nights.

More and more hoteliers are realizing that they need to start creating unique experiences, the kinds that look AMAZING on social media, in order to attract new clientele of both the boomer and the millennial variety, leading to an explosion in experiential travel.

At the California Association of Bed & Breakfast Inns in Monterey, speakers participated in a roundtable discussion with an innovative format in which each of the 200 plus attendees had the unique opportunity to hold the floor and share a personal passion or pastime. The topics that arose were as rich and diverse as the participants themselves, who hailed from various backgrounds and parts of the state.

Afterward, the conference broke into smaller groups, each focusing on several topics to discuss more thoroughly. This interactive exercise raised an important question: What do our longtime hobbies have to do with our professional lives?

In truth, if we carefully assess our favorite avocations, we can harness their power to actually fuel our business. The beauty of centering marketing strategy on personal passion is that it's never far from the heart and is always easy to get fired up about.

What's Your Passion?

What special interests can you capitalize upon in your own business plan? Begin by joining in the brainstorm, using the following list as a springboard for your thought process. At first glance, these topics may seem unrelated to the day-to-day operations of your property, but they can (and should) become very closely linked.

Listed below are some of the most popular activities and passions to give you a starting place.

Fishing

One of the top sports in America, fishing—whether out on the wide open sea or in a quiet water hole—allows time to relax in a bucolic outdoor environment. Why not entice every passionate fisherman out there by marketing the sport on your website? Offer an invitation for a stay at your inn along with a promise to share all your favorite fishing spots along with stories of your best catches. Extend your marketing reach by creating a fishing blog on your site, adding links to local fishing establishments and to your state's Fish and Game regulations. Consider penning a fishing column for the sports section of the local newspaper, and for those of cities you draw guests from. Become their expert!

Add to Your Bottom Line

- Develop a fish and fishing themed gift shop. Everything from signs like, "A Fisherman Lives Here with the Catch of his Life," to fancy fishing mugs, themed fishing apparel with your logo, books filled with tall fish tales and of course fishing gear and tackle.

- Let your neighbors know about your fishing specialty shop and look forward to booming gift sales on Fathers' Day, birthdays, and holidays.
- Consider becoming a dealer for hard to find fishing equipment, and especially a line of high-end rods and reels.
- Offer fishing workshops and consider making a special one mid-week for beginners who would like to learn how to fish or fathers with kids.

Culinary Arts

The creative possibilities in the kitchen are endless and are oftentimes what lead us to love cooking and the culinary arts. Fortunately, this is an area rife with commercial potential, and can easily be shared with bed and breakfast travelers. Offering potential guests a sneak peek at the delicious meals they could be enjoying at your inn is a sure way to pull them on board. One classic way to do this is by offering cooking classes, for which people are willing to pay both instructional and materials fees. If your zoning allows, sell wine to accompany the culinary exploration or teach wine pairing. If you don't want to teach the class, check with your local bookstore to find authors or chefs who might be interested. You'll have fun creating your own inn cookbook or equivalent, like a set of recipe cards imaginatively packaged. Be sure to send your stellar recipes to all of the newspaper food editors in areas you draw from. Ditto to the webmasters of your local destination website.

Cook Up $$$$

- Offer fine specialty knives or high-end cookware, such as Princess House, for sale to your guests.
- Theme your gift shop around food and offer regional specialty jams and preserves, canned goods, soup mixes, sauces, and so on.
- Offer a great selection of cookbooks, both new and used (you'd be amazed how inexpensively you can buy used cookbooks and mark them up for a substantial profit, all the while indulging your passion for new recipes!).

- Antique cooking utensils, serving pieces, and small kitchen accoutrements are ragingly popular with collectors—get in on the trend.

Quilting

Quilting is an activity enjoyed by many people across all age groups. Its soothing repetition and predictable, mathematical planning (which arises as you set out to arrange the patterns) offers an ideal way to free your mind and de-stress from a long day. Share this hobby with your guests by offering quilting workshops or quilting circles.

If you have plenty of room for people to lay out materials and have multiple outlets to set up irons and other equipment, then you probably have what's needed to accommodate quilting workshops! Announce these sessions well in advance on your website to reach out to quilt-loving travelers who might be planning a trip in your area. On other quilting websites, post information mentioning your inn and its quilt-lovers decor. Finally, consider contacting a Quilter's Guild and arrange to have a quilt show at your property.

Sew Up Some Extra Profits

- Have a quilt-themed gift shop and carry lots of stunning quilts, quilted placemats, pot holders, and so on. Also stock quilting books, patterns, and magazines.
- Check for a local Quilter's Guild, craft groups, sewing circles, and church groups to work with.
- Ask your local craft store to refer quilters and see if you can put a flyer up there for a monthly quilter's meeting.
- If your area does not have a specialty store for quilting supplies, evaluate this as a retail opportunity.

Canoeing and Kayaking

Water sports can be enjoyed solo or in groups, avidly or casually, and by all types of people. What better way to get in touch with the natural world! An afternoon on the river, lake, or ocean aboard a canoe or kayak provides a glimpse of the world from a different vantage point. If you're near a state park with waterways, market your inn by dedicating a special section of your website to these outdoor activities and describe all of the wonderful fun that can be had aboard a canoe or kayak. Consider renting or lending your equipment to your guests, and if you have the expertise to lead local boating trips, then by all means do so—it can only add to your inn's marketability. (Note: Make sure your insurance covers this.) Be sure to contact sporting good outfitters in your area of draw and let the folks there know that you welcome boaters.

Feature All Things Ducky

- Make your gift store the go-to place for waterway maps, cool-boating apparel, and last-minute necessities like sunscreen and sunglasses.
- Consider becoming a retailer for specialty canoes and kayaks and their accessories.
- Speaking of ducks—ducks are a favorite mascot of the boating world and have a ready market. Consider becoming "the" place for decoys old and new which are highly collectable.

Bird Watching

Bird watching gives you an opportunity to explore your natural surroundings and observe wildlife, often without even leaving the peaceful confines of your own backyard. Reach out to nature-loving travelers and share with them the distinguishing characteristics of the different bird species in your area, then challenge them to step out into your garden to see if they can spot any among all of the branches and leaves! As encouragement, include on your website a handful of snapshots of birds that you've spotted yourself. This is a natural and very easy hobby to tap into if your inn is located on a flyway, and even better if you're on a public open space or park. Research the topic to find bird watching speakers who may have written articles on the subject and see if they might be interested in coming to make a presentation at your inn. Park rangers in your area may also offer birding walks guests could join. This could easily become a whole weekend or several mid-week days of fun and learning.

Watch Your Profits Take Flight

- Stock your inn's gift shop with birding guides, binoculars in various price ranges, and bird-calling whistles.
- Commission a local craftsperson to make custom birdhouses just for you!
- Stock your inn and its rooms with bird-themed collectables, whether it's antique plates decorated with bird images hanging on guestroom walls (with a discrete price lists on the back of the door) or beautiful calendars, postcards, bird art, cups decorated with images of our feathered friends, and a line of hats with your logo perhaps a bird applique.

Gardening

If you've gotten in touch with your nurturing instincts and discovered the meditative experience of tending a garden, share the fruit of your hard work with your guests. Beautify your property with flowers or liven up your kitchen with fresh fruits, vegetables, and savory herbs. Develop and capitalize upon a specialty, such as propagating and selling bulbs and be sure to bring attention to that specialty by offering gardening classes, which are perennially popular. Contact the garden editor at your favorite regional publication and offer to write a column or run an ad for your gardening-themed getaways.

Turn Over Fresh Income

- Cultivate a garden-themed gift shop showcasing your favorite gardening publications, fanciful hats, and high-end gardening gloves.
- Sell your very own bulbs and other starts and seeds that let guests take a piece of your paradise home with them.

Takeaways

- Look hard at what features brought you to the area. Are there others who might share that interest?
- What do your current guests rave about in terms of experiences and hobbies pursued during their stay?
- What kinds of other business in your area are booming? Art galleries? Wineries? Outdoor gear suppliers?

CHAPTER 4

Setting a Price

Setting a price can be a fraught decision for many independent lodging owners but it needn't be! Just a few guidelines and the knowledge that prices are meant to change should assuage your worry and with a little experience you can become very adept at this!

As my friend Donna Massey of Palmer, Alaska once told me when I asked her how she achieved the highest occupancy at her five-room bed and breakfast season by season and over a long stretch of time, she said, "a rational common sense approach on setting prices and a friendly but low key and unobtrusive innkeeping style are my secrets." She continued,

> We believe the international Bed & Breakfast industry was founded on the principal of "perceived value," something a segment of our country's industry seems to have forgotten. If increased occupancy is your goal, we suggest an honest appraisal of rates. We have focused on volume at reasonable rates and have a six-year history of very high, year-round occupancy with a solid base of repeat and word-of-mouth clients. Our guests leave very pleased because they perceive have received more value than they have paid for. We are pleased because we have few, if any, empty rooms.
>
> We are not a destination unto ourselves. We are simply a great place to sleep when people visit our area, and we price ourselves accordingly. Just a few years ago, people would make a reservation without even asking what the total cost would be. Those days are long gone, but we are surviving and thriving because we have established our reputation for good value and prices. During busy seasons we could charge more, and people would come because there is nowhere else to stay. However, our guests come because they want to stay here. That is what gives such positive local and national word of mouth advertising. And that is what builds guest

loyalty. Give value, and you are actively marketing with every guest.

So how *did* she set those prices? Well, she called all competitive lodging in all categories motels, small resorts, home stays, and so forth located within a half-hour drive and simply asked whoever answered the phone what their charges were and for what amenities and how busy they were. By keeping diligent notes she was able to compile changes from season by season by property. These days a simple look at the competitors online may suffice, but calling and checking for promotions or getting the actual price, direct from the property adds an additional layer of knowledge.

> I looked at the few in the Palmer area and if I wanted consistent business, I needed to be close to their rates. Then I looked at rates in hotels like Quality Inn, La Quinta, Comfort Inn, Rodeway, and Holiday Inns across the nation, not just in the hot spots, I wanted a realistic picture of what the average traveler wanted to pay per night. I knew the largest segment of my market would not be dedicated B&B but the general traveling public. That led to what I believe is THE KEY to our success—that wonderful phrase "perceived value."

Donna's clear vision and rigorous good sense brought her to the top of the playing field. After collecting the competitors' rates she then laid out a chart to see how location, amenities, and aesthetics affected price and took a look at how her property fit into the equation. She then reduced the price by 5 to 10 percent—her way of guaranteeing that her value was unbeatable. Her reward for all her hard work and data collection was an enviable occupancy rate during all her open seasons and a loyal returning guest base who did much of her advertising for her by recommending her inn to others. Her savings on advertising and consistent occupancy easily made up for the 5 to 10 percent reduction in price.

Donna also knew the effort it would take and really put in the time to analyze and think about her core clientele. She set about giving them what they most wanted based on her notes left in the guest book, comments from guests, and networking with those staying in her beautiful Alaskan Bed & Breakfast.

Takeaways

- What are your property's features? Is it located near a town center or out-of-the-way? Make a list of common hotel features and check off what you have.
- Find out what similar properties are listing their rooms for online. How does your price compare?
- Be flexible, and use dynamic pricing that is, make sure you can adjust your prices across the board and across your outlets on short notice.

CHAPTER 5

Demographics Make a Difference

According to the World Tourism Organization, we exceeded 1 billion international travelers in 2014, and by 2020 over 2 billion people will travel internationally, many of them stemming from and traveling to new and growing markets such as SE Asia, Africa, and the Middle East.[1] Tourism now more than ever is characterized by globalization. These travelers want authentic, inspirational experiences and increasingly rely on mobile travel distribution. New mobile only booking sites (such as "hotel tonight," "now,"), the new sharing economy (Airbnb or Uber), and apps from major airlines and operators specifically designed for your mobile phone all make planning, evaluating and executing your trips from the palm of your hand easy. These changing traveler demands make the need for relevant content and specific target marketing crucially important.

While this chapter mainly focuses on the leisure market, a brief look at the size of the business market is helpful for further discussion. Around 40 percent of all U.S. travel is for business and 59 percent for leisure.[2] According to the American Hotel and Lodging Association: The typical "business room night" stay is by a male (64 percent), age 35 to 54 (52 percent), employed in a professional or managerial position (61 percent), earning an average yearly household income of $127,000. Typically, these guests travel alone (77 percent), make reservations (96 percent), and pay an average of $143 per room per night. The typical "leisure room night stay" is by two adults (54 percent), ages 35 to 54 (43 percent), and 55+ (32 percent), earning an average yearly

---

[1] World Tourism Organization. Compendium of tourism statistics 2016: data 2010–2014. World Tourism Org, 2016. Print.
[2] American Hotel & Lodging Association (AHLA) www.ahla.com

household income of $96,000. The typical leisure traveler also travels by car (82 percent), makes reservations (94 percent), and pays an average of $123 per room per night.

Through market segmentation we can divide the market into meaningful subgroups that will ultimately allow lodge operators to more adequately offer programming for existing customers and attract new guests, as well as understand what markets are currently underrepresented. The most commonly used demographics include, age, gender, education, and income.

Sociodemographics Age

Age cohorts have been one of the most common demographic predictors. In general, we look at the following cohorts:

- *Mature World War II* People born before 1946
- *Baby boomers* People born between 1946 and 1965
- *Generation X* People born between 1966 and 1980
- *Generation Y* or *Millennials* People born between 1981 and 2000

The baby boomer generation is obviously a good target market as they are a big cohort, control a lot of the wealth, and have time and desire to travel. People are living longer and staying more active. Target this audience by offering experiences that are different from their daily life at home, such as wine tastings, cooking classes, or other activities such as bike rides or hikes that help boomers feel young and keep learning. "The Prosperous Retirement: Guide to the New Reality" by Michael Stein further highlighted the importance to further segment the baby boomer generation into three distinct phases: the "GOGO," the "GO SLOW," and the "No Go." For obvious reasons, the GOGO niche represents a lucrative market for small independent lodges and hotels. They are still very active, in their 60s and 70s, will drive or fly and have flexible time which makes this an ideal market for mid-week or off season bookings.

Gen X is generally raising kids and most likely a little more restrained in time and discretionary spending due to mortgages, car payments, and

raising children. Social media presence is obviously tremendously important when targeting Gen X and Gen Y markets. Having free reliable Wi-Fi
is also very important for these travelers.

Millennials are another strong cohort to consider, and at 83 million
strong they have surpassed boomers as the biggest group. They take an
average of 4.2 leisure trips a year,[3] which makes them more prone to travel
than boomers and they show more interest in traveling abroad than any
other generation. In terms of age cohorts, millennials have been found to
prefer diverse hotel and travel experiences. They want an authentic and
unique experience that independent lodging can provide.

Gender

More women are starting to travel for business and this trend is
continuing. Women have also been found to value different features than
men. Women look more at the aesthetics of lodges, value security more
and also are more concerned about pricing than men. As more women
also travel for leisure, the need to cater to them becomes more important.
Studies have shown that women care more about visual cleanliness, extra
room amenities, sustainability, visually appealing marketing material and
healthy food options. Research on gender differences in service quality
perceptions suggests that women showed more concern for relational
aspects, while men valued functional aspects of service quality more.
Women hence look for services and room amenities and staff that makes
them feel welcome.

Psychographics

Travelers vary in their desire for unique and novel experiences. As early as
1973, Plog classified tourists based on personality characteristics. His well-
cited model included psychocentric travelers who prefer predictable travel
experiences, brand recognition, safety and security, food and services they
are accustomed to and are less adventurous in trying new things. Allocen-
tric travelers on the other hand travel for new and authentic experiences

---

[3] American Hotel & Lodging Association (AHLA) www.ahla.com

are more independent and adventurous and their focus is on the host culture, which makes them a suitable market for independent lodging.

Geography—Where Do People Want to Travel?

According to the AHLA, 20 percent of all room sales are international visitors. The main source countries are Mexico, Canada, United Kingdom, Japan, Brazil, Germany, China, and France. Most (55 percent) of American overseas travelers are visiting countries bordering the United States such as Canada (17 percent) and Mexico (38 percent). Other main destinations for American outbound travelers are Europe (17 percent), Caribbean (10 percent), and Asia (6 percent) followed by Central America (3.8 percent), while only 2.5 percent visit South America and 0.5 percent visit Africa.

On the most basic level, ecotourists generally reside in more developed countries. More specifically the most important source countries are: United States, United Kingdom, Germany, France, Australia, Netherlands, Sweden, Austria, New Zealand, Norway, and Denmark. There is some slight evidence from previous studies that travelers from Europe and Australia are more price sensitive than ecotourists from North America. European sourced eco travelers usually make their own travel arrangements, as FITs (free and independent travelers), while North American travelers usually use tour operators. It is interesting to note here that for the normal leisure market this is reversed, making European travelers more likely to purchase packaged tours. For both markets, this is changing as information is more freely available. Central America emerged as the preferred destination for North American ecolodge travelers. Within these source countries, travelers residing in urban areas are more likely to be ecotourists than travelers residing in rural areas due to increased stresses of living in metropolitan areas with little nature.

Takeaways for Marketing—So What?

So in summary, the first step is to start collecting data on your current customers if you are not already doing so. Examine information such as where they are from, how many nights they tend to stay, what activities they book and other interests they have. Also analyze data on gender and age. Then investigate if you are currently attracting the markets you would like to attract. If you find discrepancies, investigate the time and energy to develop a brand, message, and marketing campaign that will reach your target market. Specializing in only a few target markets means you can better serve these markets and develop a niche for you.

Takeaways

- Take a good look at your current guests, what age group are they? Where are they traveling from? What brought them to your area?
- Are your guests mainly traveling for business or leisure? Do any professional groups stand out? A proliferation of educators, tech workers or accountants?

Check in your guest records carefully. What are your biggest draws? Be sure to go back a few seasons.

CHAPTER 6

Increase Sustainability, Increase Appeal

Ecotourist Market Description

Definitive, current studies of ecotourists are hard to come by. Taking this into account, the following overview is based on several World Tourism Organization (WTO) and International Union for Conservation of Nature (IUCN) studies and the direct observations of the authors and contributors to this book.

According to Professor Carolin Lusby, when examining the demographics of ecotourism, in the 1980s males were overrepresented as ecotourists. In the mid-1990s a feminization of ecotourism took place suggesting more females engaging in ecotourism. However, gender differences are still apparent in certain ecotourism activities, with more males participating in challenging, physically active experiences. Studies have further shown that ecotourists are older than general tourists. The nature of the specific ecotourism activity offered also seems to be correlated to age, with wildlife watching activities attracting older ecotourists and younger participants engaged more often in physically demanding activities. Several studies showed the average age of bird watchers to be between the ages of 50 and 60. Furthermore, older guests tend to stay in more remote ecolodges. Studies have consistently found that ecotourists tend to be well educated, achieving higher education than general tourists. Not surprisingly, ecotourists also generally have higher income levels.[1]

Hard and Soft Ecotourists

When examining the ecotourism market based on behaviors and motivations, a classification of ecotourists along a continuum from hard to

---

[1] American Hotel & Lodging Association (AHLA) www.ahla.com

soft became apparent.[2] A "hard" ecotourist will travel for longer periods of time; prefer a deep, even challenging interaction with nature, travel in very small groups and require very little services and facilities. Hard ecotourists have a strong environmental commitment and make their own travel arrangements. Soft ecotourists on the other hand prefer a shallower interaction with nature, travel for shorter periods and in larger groups and might just add ecotourism as one part of a bigger trip. They have less environmental commitment, preferring more comfortable facilities, expect guides or interpretation and prefer to be less physically active. They generally use tour operators or agents to book their travels. Soft ecotourists are often resort-based tourists engaging in one ecotourism activity while on vacation. Structured ecotourists have the environmental commitment and activity preferences of hard ecotourists but share a desire for services and interpretation as well as comfortable facilities with soft ecotourists.

Psychographics

Psychographics include values, lifestyles, and attitudes to better understand a specific market and why they buy. Ecotourists traveled for new and adventurous activities while the general traveler preferred more sedentary activities.[3] Examining setting preferences, ecotourists not surprisingly sought out outdoor and wilderness areas, while general tourists preferred more modified environments such as cities and resorts. Specialization theory[4] is another psychographic dimension which could be useful in understanding ecotourism market segments. Specialization theory suggests a continuum of behavior based on setting preferences, equipment and skill used. Early involvement in an activity shows few setting preferences, the participant owns little equipment and has yet to develop a high skill level. As the participant becomes more specialized, the amount

---

[2] Overnight Ecotourist Market Segmentation in the Gold Coast Hinterland of Australia; David B. Weaver, Laura J. Lawton; Journal of Travel Research; Vol. 40, Issue 3, pp. 270–280; First published date: August-19-2016

[3] Fennell, D., and B. Smale. 1992. "Ecotourism and Natural Resource Protection." *Tourism Recreation Research* 17, no. 1, pp. 21–32.

[4] Bryan, H. 1977. "Leisure Value Systems and Recreation Specialization: The Case of Trout Fishermen." *Journal of Leisure Research* 9, pp. 174–187.

of specialized equipment owned increases, along with preferences for specific settings. The activity becomes central to the lifestyle or is the lifestyle, defining the social world of the participant. The take away for small ecolodges might be that more specialized ecotourists are more interested in following their activity and lodge selection is a last step in trip planning.

Tourism Queensland[5] has conducted some interesting surveys using the following definition of ecotourism:

For the purpose of this research, an Ecotourist is defined as someone who did at least one of the following activities on their last long haul holiday:

- Saw wildlife in its natural surroundings
- Stayed in the wilderness
- Visited a rainforest or jungle
- Visited national parks

And agreed that they look for at least one of the following activities:

- Environmental or ecological sites to visit
- See wildlife in natural surroundings
- Walk in untouched countryside and natural environments

And sometimes plan holidays around at least one of the following activities:

- Bird or animal watching
- Camping
- Nature, ecological, environmental, wilderness, or activities
- Walking, hiking, bush walking, rainforest walking, or rambling
- See wildlife in natural surrounds

Australia in general and Queensland specifically have a very sophisticated tourism sector and of course ecotourism opportunities abound. Reports published by Tourism Queensland examine tourist demographics from different countries. These reports conclude:

---

[5] (www.tq.com.au)

- 26 percent of tourists from the United Kingdom meet their definition as ecotourists.
- 20 percent of American tourists had the same qualification.
- 28 percent of all Chinese tourists also qualified.

These numbers are far above former estimates, suggesting to us that ecotourism worldwide might account for over 10 percent of all tourism and climbing.

Accessing the Green Market

There are three major categories of ecotourists by age: youthful ecotourists between the ages of 18 and 30 who tend to engage in adventure travel; family groups with school-age children whose parents wish to expose them to the wonders of our planet; and mature travelers over 50 and well into the upper decades who love to travel, love nature, and have the time and means to push the envelope of exploration, especially to more costly areas.

Being Green Can Be Profitable

"In Australia anecdotal evidence suggests the ecotourists spend up to 50 percent more than the average tourist and stay up to twice as long."[6]

Other studies also have suggested that ecotravelers may be willing to spend more money on their largely off-the-beaten- path tourism activities. This is certainly the case for other groups involved in experiential travel.

Some of the most direct and easily achievable impacts for business come from increased energy and water efficiency. By taking advantage of this "low-hanging fruit," many of our local businesses are seeing significant cost savings. A variety of available subsidies reduce the payback period, and several kinds of retrofits are fully rebated (including installation). Low-interest loan programs for businesses doing major retrofits for are expanding.

---

[6] (www.bgci.org)

Beyond these operational savings are the benefits from creating increased value to customers and to employees, particularly important in a tightening labor market. Various national surveys have found that a majority of Americans are looking to buy greener products, work for employers that have a good reputation for environmental responsibility, and participate in conservation programs when they stay at hotels.

Online Directories

Online directories can be a web searcher's best friend. These aggregate sites provide a tailored list of businesses with the click of a button—and all are relevant and on-point with the web searcher's query.

Most useful directories will show up among the first search engine results for their targeted search phrase. This is usually because they are well established and have built a strong reputation in the search engines. If your business is listed in a directory, you increase your chances of being found on the Web. Also, having a direct link from this well-established directory to your independent website helps to reaffirm to the search engines that your website is relevant, which helps improve your search engine performance. Try typing keywords like sustainable lodging or ecohotels and contact the resulting websites.

Sustainability Is a Three-Legged Stool

While "green" is a handy moniker, sustainability for business is really about balancing three different bottom lines: social, environmental, and financial. Any strategic decision that a business makes must take into account the effects on people, planet and profit it is to be sustained. Even within the green bottom line, there will occasionally be times when one objective conflicts with another. It's a delicate balancing act, and tradeoffs are inevitable.

Planning Pays Off

When trying to green your organization, it's tempting to take a "just do it" approach. However, like most things in business, taking time to make a plan will bring the most substantial, cost-effective and long-lasting changes.

To Go Green, Think Through All Options

There are so many ways to make your inn greener that it's hard to know where to start and how to phase and coordinate your projects and improvements so they are affordable and work together rather than interfering with one another.

For example, although increasing your inn's insulation is usually a priority, it would be a mistake to insulate a south-facing wall if you might demolish it in a couple of years so you can add on a passive solar greenhouse for a breakfast room. Or to plant evergreen trees south of that future greenhouse so they'll shade it by the time it's built. To avoid potential pitfalls, you will want to create a master plan for your green improvements. By setting short- and long-term goals and defining priorities before tearing down walls or adding expensive components to your property, you will save yourself a lot of trouble and money *and* better fulfill your goal of helping the environment.

The first step in creating a master plan is to daydream—big time. Let your imagination go and list everything you might want in an environmentally friendly inn. It's more fun if there are two or more people involved in the initial brainstorm, so long as you follow the golden rule: Never criticize or evaluate an idea during the session. Nothing kills the creative process faster than your inner judge or someone else jumping on every new idea and explaining why it won't work—it costs too much, it's hard to find the components, it might look silly, it's unproven. Just write all your ideas down as they come to you, even if one idea seems totally wild or disconnected from the others. There will be plenty of time to evaluate them. Do you want native plants? Solar hot water? A dust-free environment? A greenhouse? A graywater system? Recycled glass countertops?

Once you've listed all your ideas, you can set priorities on a cost-benefit basis that considers both. For a comprehensive look at day-to-day green initiatives, refer to the chapter on Kimpton Hotels in *Sustainable Tourism: a Small Business Handbook for Success.*

Promoting Local Art

It is also common for tourism businesses to promote local artists and craftspeople by featuring their work throughout their establishment. Local artwork is a popular take-home souvenir and offering them for sale in your business helps support local artists and craftspeople. For the ultimate authentic experience, encourage the artist to sell directly to the tourist.

In the Kitchen

A full fridge is more efficient because less cold air escapes when the door opens. Move frequently used items to the front and pack the empty space in back with jugs of filtered water.

Tossing your old cutting board and buying a bamboo one is a budget-friendly option, so buy two. Keep one for cutting meats, the other for veggies. Naturally antimicrobial bamboo is less absorbent than other materials, so they'll be less prone to bacteria. And because bamboo is a renewable resource, there's no guilt in the excess purchase.

In the Dining Room

Open the curtains. Wherever possible, use natural light to illuminate your meals, which is more flattering and costs nothing. When that's not an option, try switching your regular light bulbs for compact fluorescent light bulbs. A 25 watt pink bulb in a side lamp is a good way to warm up the color.

In the Living Room

Bird-Electron's portable speakers are made from all-natural bamboo. In addition to being much more attractive than most high-tech goods, the Japanese beauties use the natural resonance of bamboo instead of electricity. That's right, no wires. Just plug in an MP3 player or other audio device and get eco-friendly, electricity-free sound.

Nothing clears out stale or toxic air like a few happy houseplants. Recommended: Boston fern, English ivy, spider plant, and peace lily, among others, as assistants in cleaning the air.

In the Bedroom

Cover the wall with a new coat of low-VOC (short for Volatile Organic Compounds) paint which release fewer toxins into the air than regular paint. This means they're better for the ozone, and you'll be less likely to get a headache when putting on a new coat of satin latex. Low-VOC points are available from Benjamin Moore, Sherwin-Williams, and others. Use double-paned windows, and heavy draperies either lined or black-out to shut out the winter draft.

Filled fleece fabric tubes stop drafty windows and doors from cooling a room. Natural fiber bedding, towels and robes are available in cotton or bamboo and arc becoming more elegant and affordable all the time.

In the Bathroom

Jen Boulden, who is the cofounder of eco-lifestyle website IdealBite.com, says many eco-conscious hotels put soap and shampoo in shower-mounted dispensers (eliminating plastic bottle waste) and will change your linens less frequently at your request, saving about 5 percent on utilities, according to the Green Hotels Association.[7]

1. Try a low-flow showerhead: New models use about half the water of a standard one, says Dale Kemery of the United States Environmental Protection Agency.
2. Take quick showers: A bath uses 50 to 70 gallons of water; a 5-minute shower, 10 to 25. Turn off the faucet to shave and save up to 10 gallons of water.
3. Bulk up: Buy econo-size jugs of shampoo and conditioner, then refill shower dispensers so you purchase less plastic, says Elizabeth Wiatt of the Natural Resources Defense Council. Purchase more natural toiletries which are becoming available even in big box stores. Your guests and the environment will appreciate them.
4. Pick organic cotton balls: Conventionally grown cotton is assaulted with pesticides.

---

[7] www.greenhotels.com

5. Waste not: Unplug electric tools when not in use. And air-dry hair when possible-hair dryers are a huge energy drain. "A daily 10-minute blow-dry can send 110 pounds of carbon dioxide into the air in a year," says Jessica Van Steensburg of the Northeast Sustainable Energy Association.

Making Your Whole Place Greener

"A greenhouse does not necessarily mean it is full of fancy new technology."

- Reduce air leakage. Think of warm air leaking out through gaps, cracks, and holes in your home's walls and ceilings as energy dollars floating away. Sealing these penetrations is a cost-effective way to save energy. You will also notice that your house is more comfortable and has better air quality.
- Replace lightbulbs and old appliances: A compact fluorescent bulb (CFL) uses 25 percent of the energy but provides the same amount of light as a typical incandescent lightbulb. Replace an old, faulty refrigerator with an Energy Star model and you can cut your (electricity) bill by as much as 60 percent.
- Add insulation: Generally, adding insulation to the attic is the easiest fix and has the fastest return. You should have 10 inches of insulation or R-30 plus. Sustainable Spaces recommends blow-in cellulose (recycled newspapers).

Seal your ducts: In California, the average duct system has 30 percent leakage. Approximately 40 to 50 percent of your home's energy goes through this system, so it has a huge impact on your bill. Poor design and leaks mean that there is an imbalanced distribution that results in cold and hot rooms, and general discomfort. For more details on obtaining an audit, visit www.sustainablespaces.com.

In the Garden

Using sprinklers on your lawn is like throwing potato chips up in the air before catching them in a bowl—it's not the most effective way to get the job done. You can reduce your water usage by as much as 60 percent if you opt for an irrigation system over traditional sprinklers.

Try watering flowers, shrubbery, and other gardens with a soaker hose.

A Beautiful Garden That Saves Water

Xeriscaping (xeros is Greek for dry) is the practice of landscaping with drought-tolerant plants to conserve water and simplify maintenance, and it is gaining momentum throughout the nation.

With this style of low-water gardening, grouping indigenous plants together based on their water needs is important. Traditionally in xeriscaping, plants that have the greatest water requirements are planted closer to the house, and those that need little or no irrigation are planted at the lot's farthest points. For example, vegetable gardens, all of which need more intensive watering, should be planted closest to the inn and, therefore, the water source.

Five Tips for Starting Your Garden

1. Plan the xeric landscape as you would if you were designing a conventional garden. Choose native plants that offer color, texture, and shape all through the year. Group plants that need the same amount of water.
2. Prep your soil. This is key for any garden to thrive. Well-drained soil that absorbs a half-inch of water per hour will help most plants grow at a steady rate. If the preexisting soil is either too clay-like or sandy, add organic matter until the soil is crumbly when you rub it with your fingertips.
3. Install efficient irrigation systems before planting, keeping in mind that the plants closest to the house will need the most water. A drip hose can be placed above ground and mulched over or put an inch below the soil line and covered with soil.
4. Mulch, mulch, mulch. This step cannot be emphasized enough. Mulching helps to conserve water, adds slow-release nutrients to the soil and helps suppress weeds. Organic mulches usually include shredded bark, compost, and leaf mold.

5. Water for now. Even plants that eventually will become drought-resistant initially will need consistent watering until their roots have matured and are adjusted to their new home. Water an average of 1 inch per week, taking into account rainfall, at least for the first season. To figure out how long to run your sprinkler, place a measuring cup in your garden and time how long it takes to reach 1 inch. Water more when hot and less when cool.

Takeaways

- TripAdvisor has a specialty listing, The TripAdvisor GreenLeaders Program, which features properties that have a sustainable focus.
- Liaise with adventure, experiential, and agri-tourism providers to create packages that are a "natural" fit.
- Step-by-step, department-by-department, green up your products and practices in small, manageable bites.

Further Reading

Sustainable Tourism: A Small Business Handbook for Success
The Good Company: Sustainability in Hospitality, Tourism, and Wine

CHAPTER 7

Working with Associations and Travel Agents

There are hundreds of lodging associations with thousands of members. Why do innkeepers invest their money and their time to join a national, regional, or local association? What's in it for them? *What's in it for you?*

First, let's define the terms as used in this chapter:

Guest—A person who stays overnight at a place of lodging.

Innkeeper—A proprietor or manager of an inn. The innkeeper may be the property owner as a sole proprietor, partnership, LLC, or corporation. Or, the innkeeper may be the nonowner manager of the property, with contractual authority for decision making.

Inn—Refers to an independently owned small lodging property; that is, not a franchise, chain, or a flagged property. The inn may have any number of guest rooms, offer a variety of amenities, and is commonly referred to as a Bed & Breakfast, Guest House, Inn, Country Inn, Boutique Hotel, or other such designation.

Association—Local, regional, state, and national lodging associations can be categorized as having a primary mission of either marketing or professional development.

Two Main Types of Associations

Marketing-focused associations directly promote member properties through a variety of venues, including advertising and public relations. Resources are dedicated to the primary goal of bringing guests to the inns, which the lodging business succinctly terms "heads in beds" while professional associations provide education, benchmarking, plus regulatory and legislative advocacy. Education typically includes teaching innkeepers how to best utilize the venues available to put those "heads in beds."

Size matters. Both types of associations rely on critical mass, which is the number of members required to accomplish the work that the association does on behalf of the members. Whether cost-shared advertising such as a print or web directory or meaningful surveys on performance such as marketing or occupancy, membership numbers impact the association's likelihood of sustainability and the research validity. Association members therefore make a commitment not only to the association, but also to their fellow innkeepers and the hospitality industry. When assessing the value of association membership, most innkeepers recognize that they need many types of services, so it is logical to join more than one association.

An association's customer base is the innkeeper; the inn's customer base is the guest. Lodging associations work for their members by enabling and supporting the innkeeper to improve their business, keep up with changing trends and best practices.

How Do Associations Create and Provide Value for Members?

"You don't know what you don't know"

Searching the Internet on any innkeeping, lodging, or B&B topic results in thousands—if not tens of thousands—responses of wildly varying relevance. And, given the continual changes in the hospitality industry, how does an innkeeper even know what to ask?

Getting Started

The dream of owning or operating an Inn may inspire individuals to tweak heirloom recipes, fantasize about guest room décor, and then declare themselves ready to be innkeepers because they like to entertain. While delicious food and hospitality are essential, lodging associations have developed aspiring innkeeper programs to separate the facts from the fallacies—not to discourage individuals from a career in innkeeping, but rather to prepare them for reality and for success. Daily inn management often requires more time at a computer than in the kitchen, with such tasks as bookkeeping, inquiries, reservations, marketing, updating the website, social media, and blogging. The physical demands of innkeeping including loads of laundry, cleaning bathrooms and whirlpool tubs, interior or exterior maintenance of an aging historic building with aging plumbing, are not for the weak. The experienced innkeepers who typically are the lodging association's faculty for the aspiring innkeeper seminars are willing to share what must be done, when to do it yourself, when to hire it, and the software or methods available to efficiently accomplish it. Who better to learn from than the association's innkeepers who have been vetted and represent a variety of independently owned lodging properties?

Lodging associations may have specific memberships or mentoring programs for aspiring innkeepers to enable them to continue their research, learning, and search for the perfect inn to call their own.

Groups Are Smarter Than the Individuals in Them

A lodging association taps the collective wisdom and practical real-life experience of the innkeeping community on any topic of interest or question posed. The association cuts to the chase—it aggregates, curates, and disseminates the information, using tools such as newsletters, e-mail blasts, surveys, and meetings. Voila—the result is usable, tried and true help for innkeepers. Associations often provide interactive innkeeper blogs, social media groups like closed Facebook groups, online chats, and webinars to enable the immediate exchange of ideas.

Competition Versus Collaboration

Won't all this generous sharing of innkeeping secrets and expertise help the competition at the expense of my business, innkeepers and aspiring innkeepers may wonder? Let's consider the "rising tide floats all boats" principle and building a brand.

Building a Brand

Following "I never thought of it," the #2 reason travelers cite for not choosing an independently owned small lodging property is "they're too risky and I don't know what I'm getting." Enter the concept of the brand and brand loyalty.

Lodging associations establish a brand well beyond what the individual property can do. It is vital to note that innkeepers of independently owned properties individually and collectively are responsible for polishing or tarnishing that brand. This is the benefit of collaboration rather than competition.

Lodging associations build trust and establish credibility—which is their brand promise—to travelers. Guests become "brand loyal" and choose to stay only at members of a particular association: "I only stay at properties in this guidebook or on this website" or "I only stay at properties displaying a particular 'proud member of' logo." Association membership clearly provides a competitive advantage over the nonmembers. Associations wisely differentiate their member innkeepers and member properties by publicizing their standards or quality assurance programs and membership requirements in which "not everyone makes the cut." Innkeepers wisely tout their "brass"—association affiliations—through their individual marketing to differentiate their property and identify themselves as a legally and ethically operating business.

Business to Business Relationships

Lodging associations can answer questions such as:

"Where do I get those little soaps?"
"Who builds B&B websites?"
"What companies insure my property liability along with my antiques?"
"What property management systems are available for small properties?"

The innkeeping industry—specifically the independently owned small lodging segment—is very well served by businesses staffed by individuals who understand innkeeping and get the value of working with lodging associations. Associations are a link between innkeepers, aspiring innkeepers, and "vendor" businesses, maximizing the exchange of information including providing face-to-face opportunities at trade shows. Associations can often increase the purchasing power of their members through co-op purchasing or specially negotiated pricing; this is an especially valuable service for independently owned lodging properties.

Advocacy

Advocacy in the lodging and hospitality industry typically focuses on the existing or proposed regulations and legislation governing the operation and business practices of inns. Building and fire codes, food safety, ADA (Americans with Disabilities Act), zoning, signage, taxation, licensing and inspections are a sampling of the requirements placed on lodging properties.

As inns expand into new locations, the municipality unfamiliar with this independently owned small lodging type may grossly over-regulate the proposed business to the extent that opening and operating is impossible. Lodging associations are experienced at addressing these scenarios and often have established relationships with regulatory agencies and legislators. There's no need for an individual to start from scratch since associations (local to national) have mapped who or what agencies to contact, what information to present, and in what order.

Advocacy also addresses the egregious, the excessive, and the inequitable. A common example is a municipality requiring one lodging property to be licensed and pay occupancy tax while another lodging property offering the same service is not.

This scenario is increasingly more common, due to the arrival of the "sharing economy" and "short-term lodging." Websites for this lodging "niche" solicit "hosts" to advertise a room, rooms, or the whole house for rent to the public. The vast majority of these "hosts" are likely operating illegally, as they have not submitted their property to the local regulatory agencies for inspection, licensing, or zoning, nor are they insured or paying the appropriate taxes, including occupancy (room) tax. Municipalities have long regulated "short-term lodging"—defined as less than a 30-day stay—for properties such as hotels, motels, bed and breakfasts, inns, and so on, but stumble when confronted with the rapid growth of "hosts." The Internal Revenue Service (IRS) has not missed a step, as evidenced by the "IRS Sharing Economy Tax Center" which instructs "hosts" renting their property

15 or more nights annually on reporting and paying taxes for the business. Lodging associations have taken the lead in educating the public, regulatory agencies, and legislators that all properties providing lodging to the public in exchange for payment must be regulated and taxed uniformly. This "level-playing field" provides equal opportunity for all lodging properties to safely welcome guests, support and advertise the industry with occupancy tax, support community services through taxation, compete, and thrive.

When It's Time to Sell the Inn...

It's not surprising that savvy innkeepers look to the lodging association to provide education and support as they prepared to become innkeepers and as they operated their inn. But, how can the association assist as the innkeeper prepares to sell the inn? An inn can be a "lifestyle property" or a "viable business," and may involve the real estate, furnishings, and business value (goodwill, established marketing and book of business). Associations routinely field calls from persons wanting to purchase an inn. Associations often provide "Exiting Innkeeping" sessions at their conferences, and most have an "inns-for-sale" section of the website which is visited by aspiring innkeepers as they search for an Inn to purchase.

Getting Started, Operating, Exiting

Innkeepers at all stages of their career have a valuable partner in the business of owning, managing, operating, and marketing their inn: the lodging association. Whether regional, state, or national, lodging associations equip their members with the education, marketing, and tools to maximize their success as innkeepers.

Services typically provided by lodging associations*:

Aspiring (Future) Innkeepers

Education and resource venues:

- Seminars presented by association innkeepers and industry consultants

- Getting started guide, business plan development (print or Web)
- Membership—Continuing education through newsletters, online groups
- Mentoring—Pair with experienced innkeeper
- Website—Vendor listing for product and services, financing, regulatory agencies
- Inns for sale—Web list
- Research, surveys—Industry snapshot of occupancy, operations, finance, benchmarking

Innkeepers

Education and resource venues:

- Conference or seminars presented by association innkeepers and industry consultants
- Membership—Continuing education through newsletters, online groups on best practices, marketing, management, and so on
- Website—Vendor listing for product and services, financing, regulatory agencies
- Inns for sale—Website list
- Research, surveys—Industry snapshot of occupancy, operations, finance, benchmarking
- Webinars—presented by staff, industry experts or consultants

Marketing, promoting the Inn

- Standards or quality assurance program
- Website, social media (Facebook, blogs, etc.) rack-card, guide book, newsletter to the public
- Press releases, develop and sustain media relationships
- Gift certificate or card program
- Legislative and regulatory advocacy; develop and sustain relationships

Exiting Innkeepers

- Conference or seminar track specific to exiting innkeeping
- Inn consultants or realtors and financing consultants: Develop and sustain relationships
- Inns for sale—Website list

*Lodging association list by state and region: www.paii.com/Industry-Links-and-Resources

Partnering with Travel Agents

Along with associations, travel agents are there to see your property succeed.

When you partner with travel agents, you'll want to start by teaching them about your property—where it excels and who generally stays, to help ensure the right type of client is booked. This is a positive result for all parties concerned by having the travel agent set the right expectation for the client.

It is important for these small independent properties to partner with their local Convention and Visitors Bureau (CVB) and tourism boards and participate in local travel trade shows. This is how many travel agents have found some wonderful niche properties so loved by consumers.

How Do Travel Agents Work? What's Their Motivation to See Me Succeed?

Travel agents rely heavily on commission as compensation and direct business through channels that honor the time invested in qualifying and managing the sale. If you offer less than 10 percent commission, it will be a struggle to attract market-share through industry channels. On the other hand, if you pay 12 to 15 percent commission, you will immediately capture their interest.

If partnering with agents, it is preferred for the property to pay commission, but those prices should not be inflated over and above what is being offered on line at the property's book direct website. If the property is unable to afford to pay commission, then they should provide a value add-on such as a complimentary welcome amenity. Something the client would not receive if they had booked direct. If a value add-on is present, this helps the agent in charging a service fee by providing that value add-on by the property.

What's the Best Way to Go About Creating a Good Relationship with Travel Agents?

Honor the trust you build with your travel industry partners. Travel agents wield an incredible amount of influence over purchasing patterns and have the capacity to (and interest in) helping drive repeat business UNTIL you seek out direct business or bookings. Pursuing and redirecting clients from travel agents to book directly will not only damage the relationship you've forged with a particular agency, but word travels quickly in this industry and your reputation can be tarnished irreparably.

Relationships are everything. The moment a hotel sees travel advisors as a distribution channel or cost-of-sale, the hope of building anything beyond a transactional relationship is lost. Independent hotels, for all the disadvantages of not having the support and muscle that a corporate infrastructure provides, have heart, passion, and a genuine desire to serve. And these qualities mirror the travel advisor profession in spades. It's in this space that boutique and independently run hotels have the ability to forge relationships with travel advisors on a deeper level because advisors need reassurance and confidence to place their clients in what can feel like an unknown hotel, particularly at the luxury level. Ultimately, this trust isn't formed through the computerized Global Distribution System and most certainly doesn't come from a website; it's formed through human interaction and personal connections.

To zero in and cultivate advisors to support a property, hotels need to identify who is already booking their property and then seek out other like-minded agencies and advisors, and work to forge relationships with them. Put together thoughtful marketing collateral and invest the time in training your partners as it becomes a force multiplier for sales. "Help us to help you."

Never underestimate the power of the sales call and above all else, hotels need to deliver on whatever promises they make regarding the guest experience. As Virtuoso CEO Matthew D. Upchurch says, "Automate the predictable so that you can humanize the exceptional." Nowhere is this more appropriate than in the hotel space.

Things to Note

Keep in touch—Not just with your travel agents, but also with various in-person and online networks. Join local travel-focused Facebook groups and keep an eye on what they're up to. Find successful properties similar to your own and subscribe to their feed. Each property owner has unique knowledge of their property and the area where it is located. Answering questions that pop up about your area and perhaps even your hotel could build "buzz."

Lack of a standard—There is no inspector, no small property rating system. There are no real standards that must be adhered to, which can be both a blessing and a curse. On the one hand, it's this lack of uniform expectations which results in more personalized, heartfelt experience, while on the other hand, consumers don't know what they're walking into. The safer bet may be to stay at a hotel, thinks the prudent or cautious traveler. Working with an agent or agency can reassure clients that their expectations are met.

Takeaways

- Working with an association or travel agent gives you access to knowledge and tricks within the business.
- Joining an association can give any property, but especially a new one, additional presence and credibility.
- Aligning with an established travel agent, forming a relationship, listening to their advice and evaluating their feedback can give you a highly experienced, more than cost-effective guide.

Additional Resources

Association of Travel Agents (ASTA): www.asta.org

*Lodging Association List by state and region: www.paii.com/Industry-Links-and-Resources

Internal Revenue Service (IRS) Sharing Economy Tax Center: www.irs.gov/businesses/small-businesses-self-employed/sharing-economy-tax-center

CHAPTER 8

Mastering Public Relations

Top Five Tips for PR and Marketing for Smaller Hotels

Smaller hotels should put their focus on memories and experiences that they can offer and gear their marketing efforts on that. Here are five tips that will help you promote and market your property:

1. *Reward Your Guests*

   Whenever guests recommend you to their friends and family, reward them. Use a tracking service such as Flip.to, which will automatically generate the reward you're offering in exchange for guests sharing their experiences via social media. Some ideas include offering a free dessert, a free drink, or a discount at your spa.

2. *Promote Your City*

   Travelers love local, so embrace the freedom that larger hotels don't have by promoting your brand with your city or communities. Showcase local art, offer food that is sourced locally, create packages touting local attractions and events, point out secret or little-known spots and partner with local businesses that share your brand's goals.

3. *Be Consistent in Your Branding*

   Be consistent with your branding. Don't experiment with different branding throughout the year. Create a plan at the beginning of the year and sustain it for the whole year. Then you can measure how successful your strategies were.

4. *Promote Your Uniqueness*

   Determine your uniqueness or unique selling point (USP). Explore your USP, then promote it consistently in locations your target market goes online.

For example, promote your location and keep your website fresh and updated with special events, activities, and attractions that are happening within walking or close driving distance to your property.

You can also promote your restaurant and bar by organizing regular culinary events and packages such as gourmet weekends, cooking classes with your executive chef, wine tastings, and so forth.

Other areas you could promote are your spa, your architecture, design, or art collection, and your excellent staff.

5. *Don't Put Everything into One Campaign*

Create different PR and marketing campaigns for each of your hotel's strengths. For example, one campaign could target spa lovers and another could talk to foodies. And if you can, run all campaigns concurrently throughout the year. Don't execute your campaign promoting your spa one month, then jump to something else the next.

Independent and boutique properties should be marketing year-round—from their low season to their high season. Just like housekeeping, marketing happens daily.

10 Tips to Help You Develop and Work Your Own PR "Fan" Base

1. Develop a blog to post information on activities, attractions, dining, shopping, nightlife. It allows you to provide your guests with suggestion on what to do and is a constant source of content.

2. Manage your online reputation, by having guests post reviews on TripAdvisor, Yelp, and other review websites. But make sure you also respond to all reviews and that you manage and update your profile on these sites.

3. Invite guests to join your Facebook page and ask them to post pictures, videos and comments of the hotel and their trip.

4. Link local companies and attractions in your Twitter and Facebook posts by using '@' and their profile name. It will jumpstart your interaction online and grow your influence exponentially. Think like your guests. Get connected to cities, tourist attractions, and tourist information centers by liking their page.

5. Offer rewards or prizes to get the job done. An incentive gets people moving. Offer a free night in return for the best guest picture of the month.

6. Local check-in site like FourSquare or Gowalla can help you gain exposure and promote your property. Offer a welcome cocktail when guests check-in on these online sites while staying at the hotel.

7. Find interesting and funny videos of your destination and add them to your YouTube channel to create a video tour guide.

8. Reuse and recycle positive content across various social networks. Your positive reviews should be posted on Twitter and Facebook, as well as in your blog articles.

9. Get an Internet-savvy person on your team to work on social media. They will be more personal in speaking to your guests, which is very important.

10. Be funny and original. A sense of humor works better than a formal and conventional approach. It's what works.

These simple tips will help you grow your fanbase and create interaction with your guests. Engagement is not easy online, but these tips should help your hotel's social media marketing strategy.

Making the Most of a PR Agent

Word of mouth marketing is recommended in finding a good PR agent. Find a business you feel is successful, call them and ask them who does their PR and social media. Ask the local Chamber of Commerce for recommendations. Look in your local business journal.

Once you have found a PR agent you think you can work with, here are some things to consider when working with them.

1. *Ask how you can have the best client relationship.* It seems like a simple question, but some clients never ask how they can work with their PR agencies to do the best job on their account. If you're going to pay for a PR agency, why not help them succeed?

2. *Have a good product or service.* Products all have basic quality standards to meet. Cars shouldn't break down and a laptop should allow you

to do basic computing. But none of these is what make consumers enthusiastic about products. Does your product or service do anything beyond the bare minimums to be recognized in that category?

3. *Communicate*. Communication starts with meetings and calls and must continue throughout the campaign. Sharing goals and expectations with your agency early on can help them achieve your PR and growth objectives. Your PR team can do great things if they are in the loop. But what are the good things to communicate?

- Upcoming product announcements
- New company hires
- New company partnerships, big customers, and so on
- Upcoming events or tradeshows your company is attending or hosting
- Interesting things that are happening within the industry
- Anything that could be relevant to the media

4. *Give feedback.* The client needs to give the PR agency any feedback on whether the coverage is even moving the needle with web traffic, social media, conversions, sales, and so on. PR agencies can change their focus relatively rapidly if they are informed that the current PR plan needs to be scrapped, but they need client feedback.

    Also, they know you pay them to get coverage, but it's always nice to get a "thanks" every once in a while.

5. *Understand that they are the experts.* It's important that clients recognize that PR agents are the experts and that they are paying the agency to know and deal with the media. Sometimes, companies need to trust them to do their jobs—even if it isn't something that they necessarily want to hear.

6. *Be accessible.* PR reps are often at the mercy of a journalist's deadline, which is sometimes within the hour, so it's important to have access to the client at all times. Clients need to respond to media requests (interviews, images, info, etc.) in a timely manner.

7. *Realize that you aren't always going to get the big feature story.* If your company name doesn't start with Google, Microsoft, Apple, or Facebook, you're going to have to accept the fact that you might not always be the featured company in an article. The goal as PR reps is to get you media coverage that will ultimately help you achieve

your marketing and overall business goals. Companies should appreciate the company or product roundups and second-tier media coverage because it's better to be included among competitors than not included at all.

8. *Have an understanding of PR, or at least the basics.* This is one of the biggest battles PR reps face when it comes to client relationships. Unlike advertising, PR agencies cannot completely control the content or timing of coverage. Agencies inform, influence, and encourage coverage, but what comes out is up to the editor.

9. *Realize the PR agency is on your side.* Clients can forget that a PR firm wants tons of media coverage in top-tier media that drives their client's sales and web traffic just as much the client does. If they don't do a great job, they'll lose your account, which is motivation in itself.

PR and Marketing Budgets

Many industry professionals recommend you start with the industry average marketing budget. But many business successes have been contrarian. If you spend your resources like everyone else, you'll probably get average results. Breakthrough campaigns often require unusual and creative approaches. You have to decide what works for you.

Here Are Several Factors to Consider While Planning Your Hotel Marketing Budget

- Be aware of industry standards, but don't feel bound by them. As a point of reference it can be helpful to know the average prices hotels are paying for individual marketing tactics.

- Start with an Internet marketing plan for the year. If you don't know how you want to spend your money, calculating the amount will be extremely difficult. Some tactics to include are discussed in the following.

  A good budget will take into mind past results your company experienced—but will also realize that things change. What worked 5 years ago may not work over the next 5 years.

- Remember your primary business objective. Do you want more overall sales, to build your brand, or consolidate your profits? Each objective requires a different approach.
- Know your marketing priorities. Separate the "musts" from the "wants." So many things can happen along the way that cause you to deviate from a plan made months ago. Having priorities ensures the essential things get done.
- Identify which marketing strategies you really don't need to implement. There are a seemingly unlimited number of marketing tactics you could try, so identifying the nonessential helps you focus and cut costs.
- Be aware of trends, and budget appropriately. Some organizations on annual budget cycles approve money for trends way too late and miss the boat. Make sure the resources that you're dedicating to a tactic or strategy will be valid one, two or five years from now. Don't outdate yourself.

  Some recommend that hotels abandon most traditional marketing and advertising in favor of an Internet-focused strategy: 50 percent of budget for web-based communications, 50 percent for PR.
- Separate marketing costs into two categories. Initial development costs include research and strategy development, website design, content creation, marketing systems set up. Ongoing expenses and maintenance include e-mail marketing, pay-per-click advertising, search visibility improvement, website maintenance and development, consulting fees, and analytics and tracking analysis.
- Make sure that you are sufficiently capitalized. Many marketing tactics will take several months to show results, and often the best results are obtained by sticking with your marketing plan month after month—for the next 12 months. You may have to adjust your marketing plan to enable this.
- Be aware that your most important marketing investments may not even be under the traditional "marketing" budget category. At the end of the day, your guest experience is the marketing. Money you spend to create an amazing guest experience at your hotel has some of the best returns.

Think of your marketing program as an investment. If you are promoting properly, every dollar that you spend on marketing will come back to you many times over. Good hotel marketing budgets are never an expense. It's important to remember this.

The Art of the Press Release

The following tips will help you write professional, concise, and powerful news releases.

Proofread: We recommend that you write a news release in a Word or other text document instead of writing it directly on the online submit page. Writing online will not achieve the best results. Write your news release, print it, and proofread. Rewrite and then proofread again. The more time you take to do it right, the better your company's first impression.

Start Strong: Your headline, summary, and first paragraph should clarify your news. The rest of your news or press release should provide the details. You only have a matter of seconds to grab your readers' attention, so you want to capture it with a strong opening.

Identify Yourself: If you write a news release that does not identify the source of the information and news within the first few paragraphs, you may lose the promotional value your release can provide. Readers want to know who is talking. Letting them know builds the credibility of the release and promotes your name and brand online.

Write Professionally: It takes only a few sentences to discern whether a news or press release is written professionally. If your release contains hype, slang, excessive exclamation points, or direct address, chances are it will be viewed as an advertisement rather than a news release. There is no better way to destroy credibility than to distribute a release full of hype.

Answer the Tough Questions: Not everything is news. Your excitement about something and its availability does not necessarily mean you have a newsworthy story. Think about your audience. Will someone else find your story interesting? Answer the question, "Why should anyone care?" When you write a news release, make sure it contains news values like timeliness, uniqueness or highlights something truly unusual. Try to void clichés such as "customers save money" or "great customer service." Focus on the aspects of your announcement that truly set you apart from everyone else.

Pick an Angle: When writing a news release, pick an angle that will ensure the announcement is timely. Make sure that your release has a good news "hook" or angle. Tying your news to current events, recent studies, trends, and social issues brings relevance, urgency, and importance to your message.

Use Anchor Text and Features: PRWeb news releases can accommodate multimedia files like images, video, links, and other features that will capture the attention of your readers and highlight your news. Attach logos, head shots, product shots, photographs, audio files, video files, PDF documents or any other supplemental materials that build up your release. Using anchor text and hyperlinks to point readers back to your site ensures both your website and your important keywords receive simultaneous promotion in your news release.

Illustrate the Solution: Use real-life examples to illustrate how your company or organization solved a problem. Identify the problem and why your solution is the right solution. Give examples of how your service or product fulfills needs or satisfies desires. Using real life examples powerfully communicates the benefits of using your product or service.

Don't Be Afraid to Promote Yourself: Online news release distribution is a successful way to create expert status. If your company has reached a milestone, celebrated an anniversary, hired a new president, experienced significant growth or received an award, tell the world what you did right.

Don't Give Away All Your Secrets: If you're running a new promotion, tell readers where they can go to learn more. When you write a press release, provide links directly to the page on your website where readers can learn the specifics about your news and then act upon it. If you give your readers no reason to click through to your site, they're not necessarily going to.

Stick to the Facts: Tell the truth and avoid fluff, embellishments, hype and exaggerations. If you feel that your press release seems sensational, there's a good chance your readers will think so too. With so much information available to the consumer, readers are naturally skeptical. If your story sounds too good to be true, you are probably hurting your own credibility. Even if it is true, you may want to tone it down a bit.

Use Active Voice: Verbs in the active voice bring your press release to life. Rather than writing "entered into a partnership," use "partnered" instead. Do not be afraid to use strong verbs. Writing in this manner helps give life and energy to your release, which may set it apart from the rest of the pack.

Economize Your Words: Wordiness is distracting, so try to be concise. In addition, news search engines sometimes reject news releases with overly long headlines, excessive lists, and high overall word counts. Eliminate unnecessary adjectives, flowery language or redundant expressions such as "added bonus" or "first time ever." Make each word count. If you can tell your story with fewer words, you'll have better results with your readers and search engines.

Limit Jargon: Jargon is language specific to certain professions, industries, or groups and is not appropriate for general readership. While a limited amount of jargon is required if your goal is to optimize your news release for online search, the best way to communicate your news is to speak plainly using ordinary language. Using an abundance of technical language and jargon limits your reading audience.

Takeaways

- Social media must be utilized and a web presence is not optional.

- Good customer service is key. Every guest is an opportunity to get a repeat customer and spread word about your property.
- Press releases should be: professional sounding, engaging or interesting, and get to the point!

The author of this chapter said this, how do you want to handle it? "I don't have any specific references. As a PR person you should be continually scouring the Internet and reading blogs and everything you can get your hands on.

Daily I read the NY Times, Wall Street Journal, LA Times, SF Chronicle, Huffington Post, Social Media Examiner. I recommend people find their area of expertise and follow the blogs that pertain their area. These are great blogs for social media." www.socialmediaexaminer.com/top-10-social-media-blogs-the-2016-winners/

CHAPTER 9

Guest Communications—
A Bird in Hand

Once you have acquired a new guest, how do you keep them coming back for more? We will dive into this topic and discuss five ways to ensure we keep our bird in hand and happy as a lark.

Most independent, small lodging properties do not have a full-time or even part-time support staff to carry out sales, marketing, or PR initiatives. Owners are too stretched; it's a lot to run a small property with little support, so it's understandable why guest communications fall short once the guest leaves your property. This is where technology and AI (artificial intelligence) needs to work in your favor. A superior technology platform is not only going to log the guest transaction and note why the customers came to your establishment, but it should automatically follow up on your behalf with no additional action on your part (other than scheduling the frequency of the e-mail follow up and personalization). Whether you have this caliber of technological support or not, it is also possible with a simple series of personalized e-mails, regular blogs, e-newsletters, and even print correspondence to ensure customers come back time and again.

So how do we keep this bird in hand?

1. **Log all guest preferences and spend history.**
   Ideally your PMS (property management system) logs guests' data the moment the guest makes the reservation asking for detailed information to help personalize their stay. Sending an e-mail several days prior to arrival should then be easy. Whether your PMS does this automatically or not, a templated e-mail that gets the guest excited about their upcoming stay is the goal (with as much personalization as possible). In this e-mail, you can communicate check-in

procedures and other housekeeping items, but more importantly, this is an opportunity to get the guest excited, possibly upsell to a suite, add on a special lunch or massage package (20 percent off if booked before arrival), share a bit about the local area and highlights they should not miss while staying at your property. The guest life-cycle begins the moment the guest finds your property and books, growing with each interaction and your continual follow up. Per the Harvard Business Review, customers who had the best past experiences spend 140 percent more compared to those who had poor experiences. Happy guests are golden, let's not let that wear off! Following up is key to keeping this bird in hand.

2. **Be responsive.**

This starts during the guests' stay as you are responsive to their needs and learn more about the individual. Equally important is how responsive and attentive you are after the guest leaves your property. Thanking the guest for their stay and making a personal comment or compliment is uplifting and sets your property apart from the neighboring cookie-cutter hotel or motel that does little to follow up with authentic interest. Make sure to wish the guest safe travels and share that you're looking forward to their next visit. Remind the guest why it was so great to have them at the property (as much personalization as you can muster) and how you'd like to welcome them back again, sooner rather than later. I have seen some properties send an immediate thank you card in the mail (very rare nowadays but highly effective) with an upgrade voucher for their next stay (brilliant!). I have seen other properties send a personalized mug or hand towel, even chocolates (of course, you must get permission to correspond which you can secure upon check-in or checkout). The key here is to continually grow the relationship and stay close to the guest even when they are no longer on premise. If you cannot physically send an item, compelling offers via e-mail work, especially if they exude thankfulness and generosity. Make sure to include a link to TripAdvisor or other online rating programs to promote your property and when the rating is received, send an e-mail thanking them with a special offer the next time they book (make sure to include a link to your property's website).

3. **Stay in the eye of the traveler.**

   Staying in front of the traveler means being visible in locations where they frequent. Regardless of the content in an e-mail to the guest, make sure it's mobile friendly (otherwise most guests cannot properly view your offering, news, or updates). Many travelers now prefer online travel agent sites and digital communications (social media) to human interaction. You can still be highly personal, just consider where the guest is looking for properties and make sure you're at the party.

4. **Create news and happenings.**

   You are your best advocate for your property and location. No one knows your location and timely events better than you do and it's your job to keep your past guests informed. Creating buzz and PR for your property can start with something as simple as a monthly blog which then gets incorporated into your monthly e-newsletter. Aim to create a sense of urgency with deals and specials.

   This must be done delicately, in such a way that the guest is encouraged to return to your property while the special is valid. Include a quarterly calendar with events, highlights, and offers at your property on your website and in your newsletter. For example, during a lower occupancy time frame, incentivize with packages that take the guest away from their day-to-day lives for no particular reason other than rest and relaxation with a spa package or romantic weekend getaway. Piggyback on a local event in your area and pair your room with the event. Make the special available until just a few days before the event to create a sense of urgency. Breaking your offerings down by quarter is realistic and not overly time consuming, yet creates ongoing interest and value to your past guests without becoming overwhelmed to you or them. Relevant blog content with references and links to events and businesses in your area is a Google magnet but also news to fill a portion of your e-newsletter to past guests. Add in a few timely specials, photos, and news from the property, a recent quote or two from a guest, a featured breakfast item (including the recipe is always appreciated and ranks high in guest interest) and your e-newsletter is prepared.

   When sending to past guests, make sure the guests' first name is in the introduction with a unique, positive introduction each month. If there is no major news in your area, then you create the news! Your property can certainly be the center of events and local happenings generating more interest from locals and press in your area with further reason for guests to return.

5. **Cultivate loyalty.**

Whether a large hotel or a small lodging property, creating loyalty stems from personalized service and exceeding expectations. Do those two things and you're golden, then remind the guest and repeat. Loyalty programs that encourage the guests' continual use and return are great and especially popular with Millennials.

There are many ways to create loyalty, but going the extra mile is by far what's going to have the biggest impact. If your PMS logged the reason for a guest's first stay, such as an anniversary, then message your guest with adequate time so that they may rebook their next anniversary celebration. Let the guest know how honored you were that they came the previous year and how you'd like to help them make their anniversary special again with complimentary chocolate covered strawberries or a bottle of bubbly.

There are so many ways to get creative with guest communications at each stage of the guest life cycle. Consistency, generosity, and personalization are the foundation. Guests are looking for experiences, not just a bed to lay their head. By engaging your customers and exceeding their expectations you are creating a personalized service and lasting impressions that will dramatically set your brand apart. You are cultivating loyalty that will go well beyond the first night's stay. Guests will become your own personal marketing team, sending family and friends your way for many years to come.

Treat the bird with love and kindness and it will always come back to your hand.

Takeaways

- Assiduously maintain your guest database by using a great property management system to keep track of guest info, saving you a lot of time.

- Message your guest list monthly or quarterly with a timely, informative newsletter (electronic or post) and include specials and upcoming local events.
- Personalize the occasional message designed to bring back past guests, using data you gathered during their previous stays.

Resources

Examples of Property Management Systems for Independent Lodging Establishments:

Little Hotelier (www.littlehotelier.com)
Rezovations (www.rezovation.com/)
Think Reservations (http://thinkreservations.com/)
RezNexus (https://resnexus.com/)
Guest Centric (www.guestcentric.com/)
Possible Loyalty Programs suitable for Small Lodging Establishments:
Stash Hotel Rewards (www.stashrewards.com/hoteliers)
Select Registry (www.selectregistry.com/select-rewards)

References

Harvard Review: https://hbr.org/2014/08/the-value-of-customer-experience-quantified

TripAdvisor: www.tripadvisor.com/TripAdvisorInsights/n2134/video-power-management-responses-guest-reviews

PART II

Web-Based Marketing

CHAPTER 10

Website Fundamentals for Innkeepers

The cornerstone of inn marketing is the inn's website. The goal of the site is to convert website visits into reservations. Before the process of great website design and marketing can begin, you need to have some solid building blocks in place. These include your inn's name, domain name, and branding.

Naming the Inn and Picking a Domain Name

1. If you are taking over an existing inn, don't change the name. An existing inn has established marketing, web traffic, backlinks, domain history, search engine marketing, reviews, and social media following. Furthermore, Google Local relies on Name, Address, and Phone number (NAP); changing the name confuses your Google Local listing as well as the Yellow Pages (DEX) and 30 other directories. Established listings like these are important and give your site credibility. Changing the name means starting from the very beginning and throwing away years of previous work.

   Helpful hint: When you buy an existing property, be sure to get usernames and passwords to all existing social media accounts. Tracking these down after the newly retired innkeeper is vacationing in Barcelona won't be an easy task.

2. When creating a new inn, pick a good name. Research is key to this task. Look and see if there is already an inn or inns with that name or a similar one. An example of something to stay away from: anything with the name "rose" in it. There are literally 3,010,000 results for "rose inn" on the Internet. Why should that matter to you? If you use "rose" in your name, you will be competing with all those other

indexed pages for placement when a guest is trying to find you. Find something unique but easy to remember.

Do not use your surname as your inn's name. This hurts resale value. New owners may not want their inn named after you and, if they are savvy, they will know it is a bad idea to change it. Naming an inn after a historical figure or whomever built the building can be okay, just be sure to research it for competition, as mentioned earlier.

3. Once you have decided on the inn's name, you will need to determine if the domain name is available. Your domain name is your website's Internet address. Search for the availability of your domain name and what variation might be available by using the www.whois.com website. Pick something that is short, easy to spell and remember, and that includes your inn name or location. Avoid using hyphens because they can cause confusion and make it more difficult to give the web address verbally.

4. Logo design, branding, and personality are key features to your inn's marketing success. A logo is more than a picture next to the name of your business. It is a symbol that represents your inn across all media: from your inn sign outside, to your website online. When branding your business, consistency is key. All of your marketing should represent your brand (your inn's personality). Logo design, print work, and website design should all have a sense of belonging to each other. Branding your business is far more than having a logo, or even setting up standard fonts and colors. What you're striving for is having your guests, customers, and website visitors remember your business' personality. That means your marketing efforts need to speak with the same voice. Be sure you understand what you want your inn's personality and brand to be, so it can be echoed in all your marketing.

Building a Website or Understanding an Existing One

The goal of a website is to attract visitors and convert them to bookings. Four major factors should be considered when building a website or understanding an existing site: website portability and ownership, responsive design, page speed, and the look and feel.

1. Website portability and ownership needs to be understood prior to signing a website contract. Some companies use proprietary software as a service. These are known in the industry as SAS sites. Many of these companies offer websites for "free" or for a monthly fee. These sites are built via templates, are hosted by the design or hosting company, and require their current server environment to function. This means you won't be able to take your website to another company, should you choose to. You don't actually own the website you've paid for. You're simply renting it. If you decide to go with an SAS site be sure you are able to manage your SEO, and that Google Analytics are included. Many SAS companies will offer their own proprietary analytics but the numbers these analytics provide are not easily measured between websites. Analytics will help you to discuss your traffic with other innkeepers and industry leaders. By using the industry standard Google Analytics, you will be able to compare apples to apples with your analytics. Remember if you decide on a SAS, the fees you pay are a marketing expense, not an investment.

2. Responsive design is a must. If the company you are working with doesn't design responsively, find a different company. Responsive design means your site will be coded to work seamlessly from desktop to a variety of mobile devices. Google holds nearly 70 percent of search market share, so when Google gives recommendations, it is important to listen. Google states that responsive web design (RWD) is its recommended mobile configuration and an industry best practice. Google prefers RWD because content that lives on one website and one URL is much easier for users to share, interact with, and link to than content that lives on a separate mobile site. RWD also makes managing your site and SEO easier, as you have one site to maintain and market. For these reasons, all websites should be responsively designed.

3. Page speed is also important to Google. Make sure the company you choose to work with tests their products with Google page speed to ensure they are meeting all of Google's page speed recommendations. Ask to see how fast the site is at launch.

4. Once you've ensured that standards are met and the system behind the scenes is what you want, it's time to have fun! The look and feel,

or personality of your website is what *sells* your experience to the visitor. It's important to capture their attention quickly while also giving them a clear picture of what they can expect at your inn. Some inns have a fun casual vibe, while others may be more traditional and elegant. Figure out who your target market is and grab their attention with a site that appeals to them, while also staying true to your inn's personality and brand.

Website Design for Success

1. Professional photos set the stage for great website design. The best designer will struggle with poor photos and your website investment will not be as worthwhile. Professional photos with attention to setting the room and the mood are a must. It's best to choose a photographer with an understanding of the innkeeping industry. If you choose to use a local photographer or real estate photographer, be sure to show them examples of websites that capture the feeling and look of what you are after. Setting the rooms is also key: fresh flowers, fires lit, and glowing bedside tables all help create a warm and inviting feel. Professional inn photographers will assist you with room staging.

2. Well written, unique content written in a conversational voice can further show your inn's personality. Providing the visitor with concise and accurate info about your inn and area also makes you an expert on helping them plan a great getaway. Unique content text that hasn't been copied and pasted from another source is important because Google penalizes sites that use content from other sites.

3. A clear site map (navigation of your website) is key in providing organized, easy-to-read information about your inn and area. Recommended top navigation includes around six links. Too many top level choices can make your site look cluttered and be too much for the visitor to process. The following is recommended as top level navigation (you can have additional pages appear as dropdowns):

   (a) Home (this can be your logo; if your logo is your home link, it is fine to have six additional top level links)

(b) About the Inn

(c) Guest Rooms

(d) Specials

(e) Event Facilities (if you offer these)

(f) Reservations (a direct link to your reservation system)

A Contact Us link is not recommended because the goal is to have your visitors click your reservation link to book a room. Having a Contact Us button only adds confusion. Instead, we suggest having your contact phone number and reservation link clearly visible at the top of your site. Your address, e-mail, and phone number should also be clearly listed in the footer of your site. Should a visitor want to contact you, they can e-mail or call, but if they want to make a reservation, it will be clear to them to click on Reservations.

4. SEO (Search Engine Optimization). SEO is a very complicated process and should be completed prior to launch by your website developer. Proper SEO requires knowledge of the optimal keywords and terms for your business and area and incorporating them naturally into your site's text.

5. To blog or not to blog? BLOG! A blog is NOT an option but a necessary tool that should be included as part of your website. Blog posts are seen as pages to be indexed by search engines. They can then be called up by the search engine via organic searches: someone looking for a property to stay at or an event to attend in a particular area. If a visitor turns to the Web to find info on the local garlic festival and you've written a great post about it on your blog, you've just gained the chance to capture that visitor as a guest at your inn. Your blog not only gives you credit with Google for providing good content, you'll also gain the respect of guests for being so knowledgeable and helpful with your area's information.

6. Include a Virtual Walkthrough—Create quality videos highlighting and explaining the property's amenities, grounds, and rooms.

7. Hosting is the final step in launching a website. Hosting is the rented space on the Internet where your website lives and is seen by visitors. It is extremely important that you choose a trusted host who will keep your site safe from hackers with appropriate security measures

and software updates on your server and site as part of your hosting package. This service is called managed hosting. If you do not choose a managed hosting company, you will need to pay for security updates or be responsible for them yourself.

In conclusion, knowing what you need and how to ask for it makes navigating the jargon-laden world of websites a far less daunting task. The insights laid out here will help you on your way to successful website marketing for your inn.

Takeaways

- Don't be afraid to hire professionals. Your website will do better in the long run if you hire someone who does websites for a living to help set up or optimize your website rather than doing it yourself. Professional photos also make a big difference, giving your property an air of professionalism.
- The most successful websites have regularly updated blogs. They keep your website current and drive traffic in.
- Before naming your property, Google search the name you're thinking of. If you've inherited a property, see what kind of buzz you already have.

Additional Resources

Mary White: Running a Bed & Breakfast for Dummies
Travel Expert blog—Peter Greenberg: http://petergreenberg.com
Innkeeping Consultants—Peter Schermann and Rick wolf https://bbteam.com
Hospitality Expert blog—Vikram Singh: Wordsofvikram.com
For SEO and Local Advice https://moz.com

CHAPTER 11

Your Social Media Presence

As the world becomes increasingly interconnected through the Internet, the vast majority of the population now expects businesses to have a social media presence. Using technology is now a part of their overall "experience." They use the Internet for pre-trip planning, sharing photos of their holidays, communicating with friends and family back home, and leaving feedback. Increasingly, travelers are distrustful of traditional, paid media and are so turning to the Internet and social media as their digital source of word-of-mouth information.

People online are talking about your business whether you choose to listen or not. By effectively managing your social media presence, you have the ability to effectively increase exposure, increase digital traffic, improve ranking results, and improve sales. It is also key to regulating your reputation management, customer service, public relations, networking, branding, and establishing your business as a worthwhile experience.

The best way to understand social media is to compare it to a networking event. Both can be very crowded, and for some, overwhelming. Imagine a networking event where everyone shouted at the top of their lungs to no one in particular. That wouldn't be a very effective pitch. A better strategy would be to introduce yourself to everyone one at a time. Social media is similar, in that you need to treat it as a community, learn about your followers, and engage with them appropriately.

A good starting place to begin understanding your online presence is by running a Google search of your business' name, variations of its name, location, and industry. How easily can you find your business? What are the positive results? What are the negative ones? Who are the ones leaving reviews? What is your targeted market?

Businesses need to find their own way to stand out, showing what makes them unique, authentic, fun, and adventurous. The long-term prosperity and growth depends very much on how others see it in order to attract people and profits.

This chapter is designed to go over a variety of topics that will create an effective social media marketing strategy. I will go over engaging content and how to use Blogging, Facebook, and Twitter in an organic method with a small team.

Blogging

Content can be viewed as the fuel that drives the social media engine and blogging is the king of content. It is the perfect forum for businesses to spread their ideas, create a community, and build a brand. Through articles, photos, and videos, blogs are a great medium for engaging customers and partners.

4 Benefits of Blogging

1. Drives traffic to your website
2. Creates a community
3. Creates free PR
4. Gives you insights into your customers with blog analytics

Getting Started

#1 Create Your Blog

As a business, you can decide to create a tab on your website as your blog or you can buy your own domain through GoDaddy, HostMonster, or Wordpress. Creating a tab on your website could be more economical and it's easy for customers who are already on your site to find. However, that's an audience you already have. By creating a separate domain, you can drive traffic to your website through creating content that people can share on social media networks. With a domain, you also have the option to specialize the page through plugins and widgets. This can facilitate sharing your content through the domain's timeline and social media buttons.

#2 Display Credibility Banners

If you have certifications, TripAdvisor widgets, awards, or membership badges then make sure to feature them on your blog. You also will want to consider creating banners to advertise special offers and events.

#3 Include an About or Bio Menu

This is a good opportunity to let potential customers know a bit about you, your company, your mission, and ideals. It puts a personal touch on what your business stands for.

#4 Create a Social Comment System

This ties into creating a community. Show your customers that you care by responding to their comments.

Listen to what they have to say by taking their words and experiences to heart and aiming to constantly improve.

#5 Utilize Social Media Sharing Buttons

By enabling buttons such as "Like," "Tweet," and "Share on LinkedIn" on every post, you will encourage readers to share your content on their personal networks and expand your reach beyond your own followers. There are plugins that can be installed into your blog site that can accomplish this.

#6 Include Engaging Photos

Numerous studies have shown that using high-resolution and engaging photos significantly drives up results.

#7 Create a Subscriber List

Giving readers the opportunity to subscribe creates a community of people who wish to engage with your business. It's a great indicator of the quality and consistency of your content.

#8 Frequency

Those who blog 16 to 20 times a month get more than twice the traffic than those who blog less than 4 times per month

#9 Tag Articles with Appropriate Keywords

This relates back to SEO. Tagging your articles with appropriate keywords will make your articles easier to find.

#10 Link Everything Up

Have links to your website from your blog and vice versa. It is important for visitors to easily learn additional information about your company.

Content Ideas

Perhaps one of the most difficult aspects for businesses to understand is what makes great content. For instance, the "list" format is quite popular of late, such as "5 Best Local Dishes to Try." It should be noted that content is not just articles, but can also include video, audio, images, PowerPoint presentations, eBooks, PDFs, and infographics. Following is a list of ideas.

- Awards and certifications
- Associations you belong to
- Green initiatives like organic gardening, solar, and so on
- Your participation in local and community events
- Staff members of the month
- Traveler's tips
- Nearby attractions and activities

- Local festivals and sporting events
- Local artisans and musicians
- Nearby restaurants
- The history of the business
- A peek into the culture and operations of your business
- Local flora and fauna
- New additions to your business, such as more rooms or a new tour

Facebook

Each social media platform has different algorithms and audiences. Although your content can stay the same across all platforms, it is necessary to use different strategies to increase your presence. Facebook, **with 1.5 billion users of which two-thirds login every day,** is by far the mostly widely used platform, and is therefore a #1 priority in many organizations' social media strategy.

Creating a Business Page

The biggest mistake most organizations make is not creating a business page. The business page is important for several reasons:

1. Both people and other organizations can then **Like** your page. If you create a personal page for a business, then other businesses cannot view, **Like**, or tag your business.
2. Business pages come with **Insights** where you can learn useful information such as your post reach, audience demographics, and engagement.
3. Business pages have the ability to schedule posts.
4. Business pages also have the ability to create customized tabs such as **Sign up** and **Book Now.**
5. Business pages have the option to pay for promotions.

To create a business page, go to the drop down menu on the right hand corner of your personal account and select "Create Page." Follow the prompts.

Interactions with Fans: Excellent customer service extends to the digital world.

It is important to respond to any comments, messages, or posts you receive in order to ***create a community*** and increase engagement. It encourages your fans to continue interacting with you, which in turn increases your page's popularity.

It is also suggested to utilize your partnerships with NGOs, certification bodies, associations, service suppliers, and local governments by communicating with them on social media.

Statistics show that posts with engaging photos and enticing texts receive the most clicks. Take high-quality photos to share (most smartphones will take sharp, clear pictures out of the box).

EdgeRank

The majority of people falsely assume that if they have 1,000 followers, then every time they post a status update, then those 1,000 followers will see it. But that's just not the case. EdgeRank, Facebook's algorithms, decides which stories appear in each user's newsfeed through a system of points.

This means that our status updates are competing with hundreds of other stories for a single show in a user's newsfeed. If your post doesn't score well, then ***no one will see it***. The more engaging a post is, the more likely it will appear in a user's newsfeed. So **sharing** receives the most points, followed by **Commenting**, **Liking**, and **Clicking** in that order.

Facebook Definitions

- **Affinity:** Measures the relationship between the user and the creator. The closer the relationship, the more likely the user will see your posts in their newsfeed.
- **Reach:** The number of followers who saw the Post on their Timeline. This number increases as users Share, Comment, Like, and Click on a Post.
- **Engagement:** The number of times a user Shares, Comments, Likes, or Clicks on a Post.
- **Weight:** Photos and videos score more points than text or links.
- **Time Decay:** As a Post gets older, it loses its points because it is "old news."

- **Fans:** Those who engage with you on a regular basis.
- **Followers:** Those who have Liked your page.

Facebook Metrics

Photos get 53% more likes, 104% more comments, and 84% more clicks	Posts with 80 characters or less receive 66% more engagement	Posting 1-2 times a day gets 40% more engagement than posting 3+ times a day

Twitter

As mentioned before, each social media platform has different algorithms and audiences. Although content can stay the same across all platforms, it is important to use slightly different strategies to increase your social media presence. Twitter is the second most widely used platform. It is known for its limit of 140 characters, which creates a micro-blogging atmosphere. Twitter has more than 9,100 tweets per second, summing up to over 1 billion tweets in just 5 days. Around 40 percent of Twitter's followers (of around 645.7 million users) are just spectators, meaning that they follow what others are tweeting without tweeting anything themselves.

Posting Frequency

Twitter is a great tool for sharing about events in real-time. It is recommended to tweet two to four times per day and retweet another two to four times per day. However, sending more than one tweet every hour is considered spammy and can significantly decrease your click-through rate.

Within this microblogging atmosphere, it is important to not just tweet at your followers, but to tweet with them. ***Connect with your community***. Follow their conversations, answer their questions, and retweet them.

Hashtags

Hashtags are a word or phrase precipitated by the # that links the Twitter community around a given topic. For example, if you typed in

#ecotourism in the search box, you'll find a lot of useful information about the subject from organizations, people, and companies such as TIES, Ecotourism Kenya, and EcoCamp Patagonia. Hashtags can also be tailored to your specific brand.

It is recommended to use at least two hashtags per tweet. Using more than that can be considered spammy. Hashtags are especially used to strategically mention important causes, campaigns, and events.

Twitter Metrics

Tweets with images have engagement rates 2x higher than tweets without images	Tweets that contain fewer that 100 characters recieve 17% greater engagement rates than longer tweets	Tweets with hashtags recieve 2x more engagement than those without

Tweet Tips for Great Content

Use Inspirational Quotes or Testimonials

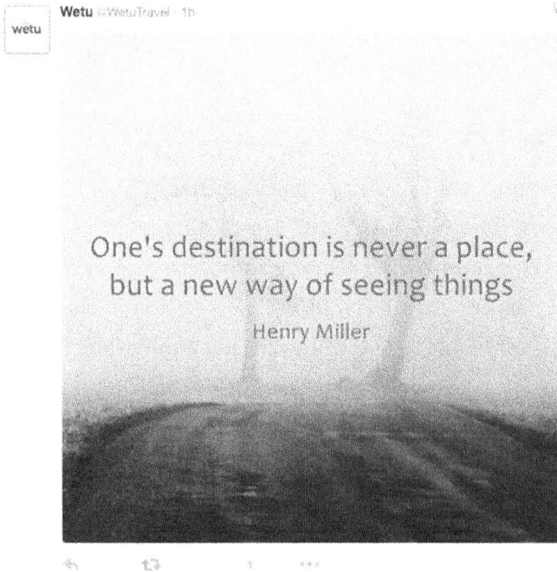

Well-Formatted, Easy to Read, and Factual Tweets

TIES ecotravel · Sep 29

Become an Ecotourist and learn 5 easy
steps to planning your trip! bit.ly/1O5SvT5
#ecotourism #travelguides

7   8

Tweets that Tap into the #BreakingNews Cycle Such as Tweeting About International Days or Holidays, for Example, the UN's World Tourism Day

TIES ecotravel · Sep 27

"Every time we #travel, we are part of a
global movement!" #1billiontourists
#WTD2015

3   6

Milestones Such as "25 Years in Business" or "10,000 Followers"

TIES ecotravel · Aug 19

International Ecotourism Society Still Going
Strong After 25 Years bit.ly/1Expo2g
#ecotourism

7   4

Takeaways

- Start where a potential client would start. Run a Google search, not of terms you think will bring your website up, but of phrases that someone searching for a place to stay might. Use well-known terms like ecolodge or B&B, start small (with the nearest town name in the search) and work your way to a wider radius.
- Facebook—Create a business page and *don't forget about it!* It needs to be checked and new content posted regularly. Answer any questions that come in.
- Twitter—Utilize hashtags and post at intervals. Rather than tweeting three times each day all in the same hour, spread them out across nine hours, posting every three or so.

CHAPTER 12

SEO (Search Engine Optimization)

Marketing Terms

SEO (Search Engine Optimization)
The process of increasing the visibility of your website in a search engine's unpaid (organic) results. Traditionally SEO applies to techniques applied to your website for desktop searches.

Mobile SEO (Mobile Search Engine Optimization)
The process of increasing the visibility of your website's visibility in mobile searches.

LSO (Local Search Optimization)
The process of increasing the visibility of your local or maps listings in search engine results, to make it easy for your prospective customers to find information about your company online.

SMO (Social Media Optimization)
The process of increasing visibility and awareness of your brand on social media outlets.

Organic Versus Local Maps Versus Pay-Per-Click (PPC)

Currently, Google makes up the largest majority of a lodging property's referrals. Bing and Yahoo are also search engines where a guest may find you online and book a room, but their market share is quite small as compared to Google. Therefore we will be using Google snapshots in the following examples.[1]

---

[1] http://stats.areppim.com/stats/stats_websearchxsnapshot.htm

Organic Unpaid Free Listings

Organic Unpaid Free Listings are the results seen displayed with a Title (top line), the URL link (green link), and a Description (Grey lettering below link). Placement of these listings are based on the website's overall online authority, which may be influenced by On-Page SEO, Mobile SEO, and a variety of other Off-Page factors.

A Note on Mobile SEO

Responsive design is Google's recommended design pattern. Google required all websites to be mobile friendly on or before April 21, 2015. Google updated their mobile algorithm again in May 2016 to further validate that sites being displayed in their mobile results are mobile friendly.

See the mobile-friendly tag in Organic Unpaid Free listings example above.

- Googles Mobile Friendly Requirement:
  https://developers.google.com/webmasters/mobile-sites/mobile-seo/
- Googles Mobile Friendly Test:
  www.google.com/webmasters/tools/mobile-friendly/
- Googles PageSpeed Insights Testing Tool:
  https://developers.google.com/speed/pagespeed/insights/

Local Maps

Local Maps listings are the results seen either in the current 3-Pack Web search or on a Map search. These listings are mainly controlled by your GMB (Google My Business) listing, NAP (Name Address, and Phone) accurateness, citations, in-bound links, and so on. Google indicates that your placement in these listings is based on Relevance, Distance, and Prominence. As of April 2016, OTA (Online Travel Agency) availability is now playing into your Local Placement.[2]

Pay-Per-Click

PPC is a paid marketing option for being seen in the search results. The lodging property engaging in a PPC marketing campaign will pay an advertising fee each time one of their ads is clicked.

Note: PPC ads can be found on both desktop and mobile, depending on how the advertiser sets up their PPC campaigns. PPC ads are notated with a small yellow AD symbol in Google.

---

[2] https://support.google.com/business/answer/7091?hl=en;http://moz.com/blog/2013-local-search-ecosystems

DESKTOP RESULTS

New Orleans B&Bs - Find Unique Rentals in New Orleans - Airbnb.com
www.airbnb.com/New-Orleans ▾
Book Bed & Breakfasts From $49/Nt!
Ratings: Selection 10/10 · Website 9.5/10 · Prices 9.5/10 · Travel info 9/10 · Service 9/10

Plan Your Dream Vacation   View most Popular Rentals
Create Your Own Wish List   Learn how Airbnb Works

B&Bs Deals in New Orleans - trivago.com
www.trivago.com/Hotels-B&Bs-NewOrleans ▾
B&Bs in New Orleans from $22 · Over 218 Hotels to Choose from!
Act Fast for Great Deals · 900,000+ Hotels Worldwide · Save Time and Money

MOBILE RESULTS

New Orleans B&Bs - Find Unique Rentals in
New Orleans - Airbnb.com
www.airbnb.com/New-Orleans

Book Bed & Breakfasts From $49/Nt!
Ratings: Selection 10/10 · Website 9.5/10
Plan Your Dream Vacation - What is Airbnb™?

B&Bs near French Quarter - Booking.com
www.booking.com/B&Bs-French-Quarter

4.5 ★★★★★ advertiser rating
Lowest Price Guarantee! Book a B&B near French
Quarter
Read Real Guest Reviews · Free Cancellation
Secure Booking - Book for Tomorrow

How to "Test" Your Placement in Google

When searching in Google, Google Localization (where you physically are located when doing the search) and Personalization (what Google knows about your searching history) will greatly affect your results.

To perform a clean Google Placement search…

Step 1: You must be logged out of your Google account
Step 2: You must clean your Cache and Cookies

Note: We suggest you choose a browser that you don't use as your daily work browser, so you don't accidentally delete any of your business passwords.

How to Video: http://www.youtube.com/acorninternet
Look for Educational Byte .009

SEO: On-Page Versus Off-Page Factors

On-Page factors are things that your webmaster should include in your website development and design. Off-Page factors are things that you need to be aware of that will impact the placement of your site.

On-Page Factors (On Your Website)

Meta Tags
Content

Header Tags

Internal Links

Publisher Tags

Rich Snippets for NAP and Geo Location (Schema)

Ongoing fresh content via consistent, quality blog posts

Meta Tag Details

Since 2009 Google DOES NOT read the KEYWORD META TAG.
Google DOES read the TITLE and DESCRIPTION META TAGS.

Example of what TAGS look like in your website code...

<title>Avenue Inn Bed and Breakfast: Located in New Orleans Garden District</title>

<meta name="description" content="Stay at Avenue Inn Bed and Breakfast, just minutes from the French Quarter in New Orleans, offering contemporary amenities with all of the comforts of home">

What TITLE and DESCRIPTION TAGS look like in the Google search results...

TITLE ➡ Avenue Inn Bed and Breakfast: located in New Orleans Garden District
www.avenueinnbb.com/ ▾
DESCRIPTION ➡ Stay at Avenue Inn Bed and Breakfast, just minutes from the French Quarter in New Orleans, offering contemporary amenities with all of the comforts of home

How Are TITLE TAGS Created?

A Unique TITLE must be written for each page of your website, including each blog post.

A TITLE is made up of a short variation on the words that make up the "theme" for that individual page.

A TITLE is inspired from the readable text on that individual page.

A TITLE is used to quickly show the user what they can expect to find on that page of the site should they click on it to read it.

The TITLE will read like a short and friendly call to action.

TITLES used to be 60 to 65 characters long. As of March 2014 they are now 50 to 55 characters for both mobile and desktop.

TITLE TAG Guidelines Provided by Google...

Page TITLES should be descriptive and concise.

Avoid vague descriptors like "Home" for your home page, or "Profile" for a specific person's profile.

Avoid unnecessarily long or verbose titles. Long TITLES are likely to get truncated when they show up in the search results.

Avoid keyword stuffing.

It's sometimes helpful to have a few descriptive terms in the title, but there's no reason to have the same words or phrases appear multiple times.

Avoid repeated or boilerplate titles.

It's important to have distinct, descriptive titles for each page on your site.

Brand your titles, but concisely.[1]

Why Does Google Change my TITLE TAGS on Some Searches?

If Google feels that your TITLE doesn't best match the individual surfers search, they will discard your TITLE and make up a new TITLE to be displayed themselves.

"Sometimes even pages with well-formulated, concise, descriptive titles will end up with different titles in our search results to better indicate their relevance to the query. There's a simple reason for this: The title tag as specified by a webmaster is limited to being static, fixed regardless of the query. Once we know the user's query, we can often find alternative text from a page that better explains why that result is relevant. Using this alternative text as a title helps the user, and it also can help your site. Users are scanning for their query terms or other signs of relevance in the results, and a title that is tailored for the query can increase the chances that they will click through.[2]"

---

[1] https://support.google.com/webmasters/answer/35624?hl=en

[2] https://support.google.com/webmasters/answer/35624?hl=en

Content Details

Write 150 words per page at the bare minimum. Google needs to be able to read content to best know how to display your pages in their results.

There is no maximum number of words per page, just make sure your content stays on point for the theme of the page.

The TITLE phrase contents must be found in the text of the page.

Google DOES NOT read images or FLASH. You MUST have words!

You MAY NOT copy or duplicate content to be used on your website or blog from anywhere else on the Web!

Your content must be original, fresh and be found only on your website alone.

Header Tags and Internal Links Details

Header Tags tell Google when something is important. These tags are coded into your website supporting your content. Example: H1, H2, H3.

Internal Links allow your user "to click to read more" about a topic as they read through your website text. These internal links are attached to words called "Anchor Text."

Example: Our gourmet breakfasts are served each morning in the main dining room between 9:00 and 10:00 am. Where the words: Gourmet breakfasts would link to the breakfast detail page.

Publisher Tag Details: Publisher tags connect your Google My Business (GMB) listing with your website.

Your Webmaster may add the Publisher code to your website.

<link href="https://plus.google.com/u/0/YOURG+LISTING ID" rel= "publisher"/>

Rich Snippets for NAP and Geo Location (Schema) Details

Local Rich Snippets allow Google to understand exactly who and where you are based on your website code. This supports your listing in the local search results.

Rich Snippet Testing Tool: https://search.google.com/structured-data/testing-tool

Use the previous link to generate an example of your website's Rich Snippet Results.

Off-Page Factors (Not on Your Website)

- Facebook Presence References
- Twitter Presence References
- Inbound Links (Local and Global)
- Citations (Local and Global)
- NAP (Name Address Phone)
- GMB Listing Maintenance
- OTA (Online Travel Agency) Participation

Off-Page Factors: Additional Influences

All these items (and more) contribute to your overall Authority and Internet presence. The site with the highest Authority typically will show the highest in the Search Engine Results.

- Age of your URL (not controllable)
- TITLE Phrases in URL (controllable) *In the distant past this was an accepted technique for supporting placement. Today if you are choosing a NEW URL it's not recommended. Learn more about Google's EMD (Exact Match Domain) Release.*[1]
- Number of quality pages on website (controllable within budget).
- Existence of spam on your website (controllable)— Example: Such as your site being hacked, and ads for unrelated products pop up on your website.

---

[1] http://searchengineland.com/low-quality-exact-match-domains-are-googles-next-target-134889

- Quantity and quality of In-Bound Links to website (controllable within reason).
- Number, accuracy, and quality of citations of your business NAP (controllable within reason)—For example: Mentions of your business name and address on other web pages, even if there is no link to your website.
- Google approved Responsive Mobile Website (controllable).[2]
- Speed and usability of website *Google's PageSpeed Insights test will tell you the speed of your mobile and desktop sites. When possible, it's best to aim for scores in Green.*
- Group sites tend to get higher organic placement (not controllable)—such as a B&B association website, directories, review sites, and so on. *If you can't beat them, you might want to join them.*
- Distance to groupings of Business Types in Google Local Maps (Not Controllable)—For example, if there are grouping of Inns in proximity, in the area you are marketing to, and how close you are to the group.
- Social mentions (controllable within reason)
- Third party reviews (controllable within reason)
- Driving directions (controllable)—Google has indicated in their GMB reports that they track the number of times a guest clicks on your driving directions. It's a feature they track.
- OTA participation (controllable)

---

[2] https://developers.google.com/speed/pagespeed/insights/

Digital Baggage

During the past decade, many different types of SEO and LSO strategies have worked quite well for gaining high placement.

Strategies that Google not only evaluated as part of their algorithms, but in some cases actually recommended, no longer work today, and in some cases cause harm to your placement.

It's not just about the SEO on your website. It's about your overall online web presence. If you have digital baggage that hasn't been dealt with, your website's placement can drop. Even with quality On-Page SEO.

Here are some types of digital baggage that can negatively impact your website's placement.

Duplicate Content
Reciprocal Links
Three-Way Links
Partner Pages
Links Pages
High Keyword Density
Targeted Anchor Text
Blogging with Text from Other Sites
NAP Issues
And the List Goes on and on…

Ongoing Marketing

Improving your online presence goes far beyond your On-Page SEO. Ongoing marketing programs should include a plan to have these items attended to on a regular basis—daily, weekly, and monthly tasks are all involved in ongoing marketing. The days of adding On-Page SEO and hoping for the best are gone. Today you MUST keep your presence up, well beyond your On-Page SEO tasks that should be completed as part of your Website design, and kept up on a regular basis when Google's guidelines change.

Someone MUST keep your online presence FRESH.
Someone MUST write SEO friendly blog posts.
Someone MUST start and maintain a social media program.
Someone MUST build quality inbound links and citations.
Someone MUST claim and maintain your Google My Business (GMB).
Someone MUST claim and maintain all major LBL (Local Business Listing) accounts.

Someone MUST review your Google Analytics for quality marketing decisions.

Someone MUST monitor your Google Console for messages from Google

Someone MUST keep on top of Google's ever-changing search environment.

Someone MUST watch your overall web presence—video, social media, newsletters, promotions, directories, local, organic, and so on. It's not just your website. It's your website and all the other supporting factors.

Someone SHOULD send newsletters.

Someone SHOULD send press releases and establish press contacts.

Someone MUST continue marketing and monitoring your online presence.

The question is: **Who is that someone going to be??**

You? Or a third party you employ?

Google Analytics Tracking

Once you've completed all your On-Page SEO tasks, verified you've cleaned up any Digital Baggage, and have established an Ongoing Marketing Plan, how do you know if all this work you've done is actually putting Heads-In-Beds?

You can't ask your guests where they found you. On average a guest will look at many different sites before deciding to book a room with you. You can't trust that information to determine what is working and what is not working with your marketing plan.

Google provides a FREE TOOL called Google Analytics. This tool, when properly installed will give you the data you need to know what part of your marketing plan is and isn't working.

But be careful. You want to make sure you are not tracking just your referral traffic. Though referral traffic is a good thing to be aware of, it's so much more important to know how much revenue is associated with that referral traffic. Are you getting bookings from Google, TripAdvisor, or a Directory (Otherwise it sounds like TripAdvisor is directory you pay for)? You need to know more than if you're receiving traffic from these sites, but if you're getting actual bookings.

In order to obtain this type of Revenue Tracking data, your Webmaster should be installing Universal Analytics with E-Commerce Tracking as part of your Google Analytics install.

Not all Booking Systems support Universal Analytics with E-Commerce Tracking, so you must ask. Keep in mind that as your Webmaster installs Universal Analytics with E-Commerce Tracking there are three separate parts they must update correctly.

- Update website: Google Analytics code and cross domain linker code must be installed correctly on all your website pages (Your Webmaster Should Do).
- Update booking software: Google Analytics code and cross domain linker code must be installed correctly in your Booking Engine (You or Your Webmaster or Your Booking Engine Company Should Do).
- Update Google Analytics Settings: E-Commerce Tracking and your Exclusions must be set correctly in your Google Analytics Account (You or Your Webmaster Should Do).[3]

Once Universal Analytics and E-Commerce Tracking is properly installed, you will be receiving quality data to help you wisely manage your marketing plan into the future that looks something like this:

Wrap-Up

A decade ago it was really pretty easy to be found in the search engines. Some content, photos, and a few meta tags and you were good to go. Today, with all the different places you can be found in the search engines, it's no longer that easy. On-Page SEO is still very important to your placement, but without all the other supporting factors, it will not work well on its own.

---

[3] https://support.google.com/analytics/answer/2790010?hl=en

Source / Medium	Acquisition			Behavior			Conversions eCommerce ▾		
	Sessions	% New Sessions	New Users	Bounce Rate	Pages / Session	Avg. Session Duration	Ecommerce Conversion Rate	Transactions	Revenue
	13,163	73.78%	9,712	40.38%	4.12	00:03:05	1.59%	209	$70,233.00
1 google / organic	4,919	69.59%	3,423	33.71%	4.66	00:03:33	2.32%	114	$39,782.00
2 (direct) / (none)	3,564	77.72%	2,770	56.00%	3.09	00:02:18	0.95%	34	$10,042.00
3 bedandbreakfast.com / referral	1,741	73.41%	1,278	18.44%	5.29	00:03:50	1.32%	23	$7,699.00
4 bing / organic	373	69.17%	258	27.88%	5.35	00:03:59	2.41%	9	$3,326.00
5 yahoo / organic	228	65.79%	150	37.72%	4.37	00:03:57	3.51%	8	$2,700.00
6 tripadvisor.com / referral	151	66.89%	101	9.93%	6.48	00:06:30	3.31%	5	$1,727.00
7 bbonline.com / referral	110	71.82%	79	9.09%	5.02	00:04:21	4.55%	5	$1,580.00
8 aol / organic	25	80.00%	20	28.00%	4.56	00:03:12	8.00%	2	$756.00
9 tripadvisor.com / cpc	86	68.60%	59	52.33%	3.41	00:04:16	2.33%	2	$656.00
10 bnbfinder.com / referral	94	69.15%	65	20.21%	5.87	00:04:35	1.06%	1	$598.00

Takeaways

- Do not take text from other sources and put it on your website. Google WILL know and WILL ding you.
- Unless you are a tech expert familiar with SEO, hire someone to handle it for you.
- You have to keep updating your site. New content is what drives traffic in.

CHAPTER 13

Tips and Tricks for Staying on Top of Your Content

Finding the time to manage online marketing can be difficult. One of the top reasons people don't keep up with it is because it has to be ongoing—new content has to be posted regularly. Not an easy task for small property owners already dealing with bookings, upkeep, travelers, and so on. Here are our recommendations to help you keep up with the demands an online presence comes with:

- *Draft your content in groups, all at once*—Get everything written at once for the next week, two weeks, or month for social media sites, your blog, e-mail newsletters, and so on and save them as drafts or schedule them to be posted at intervals. Rather than hopping on the computer to write an article Monday, Wednesday, and Friday, write three Monday. You'll find it a lot easier to get them written if you're already on a roll.
- *Automate everything you can*—The Web is awash with plugins and scripts that save you the work of doing everything yourself. Set up your blog to automatically post to your Facebook, Pinterest, Twitter, or other social platform when you post a new article to your blog. Online social media managers such as Hootsuite may serve this purpose as well.
- *Create autoresponders*—Autoresponders are e-mails that automatically get sent out when new subscribers join your mailing list or e-mail you with a frequently asked question or some such. You only have to write the e-mail once, but it will serve you long term.

Following that train, automate your newsletter sign-up field so it automatically adds new subscribers to the e-mail list. Both Constant Contact and MailChimp have plugins and scripts that you just have to install into your website.

- *Use templates*—A template is an already formatted document, e-mail, newsletter, and so on that you just have to insert your text into. Rather than spending time every time you want to send something out inserting your logo and making your content look pretty, you just have to place your words onto a page already presentable. If you're unsure of where to start, Constant Contact and MailChimp both employ templates. If you're looking for something else, you can search the Web for things like "business e-mail templates" or "template for flyer" and chances are you'll find a good place to start.

Out of ideas? Look to the open source or consider outsourcing your writing needs—The open source is a great way to find content you can use without infringing on intellectual rights or plagiarizing. Search places like YouTube and www.ezinearticles.com which have a lot of information that you can legally use.

If you don't have time for that, you may want to consider hiring a writer to keep up your web presence. You can employ someone just to write, someone to write and manage your social media and posting, even someone to take care of the upkeep for your entire website.

CHAPTER 14

The Rating Game: Leveraging Consumer Reviews

A recent PhoCusWright study revealed the impact reviews have on travelers' decision-making:

- 83 percent of respondents indicated that reviews help them pick the right hotel.
- 80 percent read at least 6 to 12 reviews prior to booking.
- 53 percent won't commit to booking a hotel room until they read reviews.

The logic behind a review then is simple. If others had a positive experience, then the traveler assumes they too will have a similar stay and feel comfortable in making a decision to spend their money on one place over another. If travelers share their bad experience, then the assumption is why would my stay be any different? While any business is going to share the very best about what they offer and tell travelers they put their visitors' needs first, the reality is that actions speak louder than words and consumers want their experience shared to help the next person.

Yelp has a very large number of Bed and Breakfasts that have reviews, yet the majority have not claimed their Yelp listings and have not responded in any way to travelers' reviews.

Facebook Business Pages also have many independent properties with reviews, yet often they go unanswered and unresponded to.

For tutorials and instructions, take a look at a site's help page. It's there for your benefit.

Note: More than 50 percent of negative online reviews either mention, or are prompted by issues with a property's deposit and cancellation policy or other issues like not replying to e-mails or phone calls, or food quality.

Responding to Reviews

Some marketers suggest only replying to negative or bad reviews. Ideally a property manager should respond to all reviews, even as simple as thanking the traveler for taking the time and care to share the traveler's thoughts about their property. The response should not be canned, instead, personalize them as much as possible. Each response should be customized to the review itself. For example, if a guest complimented the B&B on their waffles, then mentioning this in the review response shows care and attention to each individual person who will hopefully become a repeat customer in the future.

A response, while targeted to the reviewer, is primarily intended for the thousands of people that will be reading these reviews (and the owner's or management's responses) for many years to come.

By responding to reviews, both positive, negative, and in between, a lodging property is demonstrating to travelers that, (1) the property and its staff truly care about what's being said; (2) the property and staff are going the extra mile to thank the guest for leaving their review (something that is so simple yet goes so far); and (3) Showing engagement and interest in what a guest thinks and that the property values their thoughts and opinions.

Reviews have become an increasingly important part of the decision-making process for most travelers, with more and more credence given to what other people have to say about a business rather than what a property owner says about their business on their online and offline marketing. With the number of people relying on reviews to help them choose their next destination, it's essential that an innkeeper learn over time how to navigate the world of other peoples' opinions. Engagement with past guests and potentially new guests increases the chance that they will either book a B&B for the first time, or return if they had been there before. Engagement is personalization of a travel experience, and guests of all ages are finding that it makes a huge difference to them in whether a lodging establishment responds and interacts on a personal level, or just treats a guest like another number walking through the door.

By responding to a positive review a property owner is also responding directly to the reviewer and developing a deeper rapport. When a reviewer has had a positive experience at the B&B, and had their review followed up on, the likelihood that the customer will become a repeat guest is greatly increased.

Social Media and Other Review Sites

Take to heart things mentioned in reviews, as one can learn things and improve upon them. To give an example, one inn had dozens of reviews and just about every single one mentioned the "little notes," that the innkeeper had written instructions and information on -even the very positive reviews. After discovering how irritating people found the post--it notes, the innkeepers condensed all the information, and created a framed one sheet that was placed on the room door for review.

Facebook

Once someone is logged into Facebook, they can see about 80 percent of what's posted online. I am not suggesting a property stalk their employees, but if the inn has a potential problem employee, it doesn't hurt to be careful. Past issues that hospitality businesses have run into that have snowballed out of control on the media were cases like a cook saying on his Facebook personal page that that he was feeding gluten to gluten-free guests, or a housekeeper at a small resort talking about how they don't fully clean the guest rooms.

Yelp

What about Yelp? Why is Yelp important when there are sites like TripAdvisor? A few years ago, there were no reviews of inns on Yelp, now there are many more and growing. Plus, Yelp reviews get picked up by the search engines. More Gen Y age people use Yelp as a review platform than TripAdvisor, as they grow older and become more interested in the experience B&B's provide, this will be important.

Out of every review—positive, negative, or ambivalent—improvements can be gleaned if one takes a step back and does not take it personally. Especially if there are multiple people commenting about something.

How to Deal with Difficult Reviewers

Troublesome reviewers generally come in two varieties. The first is someone who may have been a legitimate customer who just had a bad day: someone taking something the wrong way, or someone who called didn't like what a business had to say and decided to take their frustrations out online. These individuals don't go out of their way to be troublesome, they just... are.

The other group is differentiated by their malicious intent. They WANT to ruin your day. You may have heard the term "troll" before if you've spent time online, which stems from their penchant for "trolling" the Internet looking to rile up or upset strangers online. They may exaggerate, lie, or just be generally nasty. We'll talk about how to deal with this group first.

If a "troll" has posted a review on a major review site, such as TripAdvisor, Yelp, and Google+, you still have to pay attention to it. These sites won't remove the reviews so you have to respond. A troll's aim is to get a rise out of you, so that is exactly how you won't respond. Don't get upset, don't get aggressive or give in to the temptation to be snarky right back. One of the best ways I have seen to deal with troll reviews is apologize and then say, "We have looked through our records and can find no record of you being a customer. Please contact us so we can clear any issues up you think you might have had." You know they'll never follow up so asking them to call to clear the air is a good strategy.

You aren't responding for the sake of the troll, but for the future potential guests who will see the review and the management response.

On to the "bad day" reviewers.

This group is more easily dealt with, but again, the key is that you do actually need to respond. Sometimes these reviewers can sound a little unhinged, know that other readers can tell. In the case where it *is* a normal customer just having a really bad day, a business will want to try to bring that customer back and give their business a second chance.

Maybe you don't want customers like that back, but how many people is that unhappy customer going to tell about their experience if you don't make the effort to try and address or remedy the issue?

One of the best responses when dealing with someone like this is: "This is the owner (or manager), we are sorry you had an unpleasant experience, please contact us so we can discuss any customer service problems or any other issues you might have had, thank you." Adding something like we are dedicated to being a customer-service oriented lodging doesn't hurt either.

Don't get defensive, don't disagree with, or tell them they are wrong, and don't say they misunderstood or that they were mistaken. An unhappy customer treated disrespectfully can easily turn into a troll, and an on edge customer can turn into an even angrier one. Don't let a situation evolve into one that's even worse.

A reviewer who is a bit off kilter will generally let it go. When it happens that a guest was inebriated (and it does happen), most often they will apologize to the business owner and remove the review. The "bad day" customers can turn into positive evangelists for the property but it will take strategic communication and care to get there.

And again remember, the primary aim of responding to difficult reviewers is not for them, but for all the other potential future customers reading the reviews and the responses.

Additional Tips

If there is a mention of any type of injury (including food poisoning) do not make any mention of it in the review response. In this sue happy society, any mention of such, truth or not, can be used as an example of guilt.

Never make any mention of any kind of reimbursement or restitution for an issue, as that is to be settled privately (if they are a legitimate guest or past guest) and posting of such information only encourages those looking to get something out of it.

Don't offer incentives for reviews, it's against the terms of service of most platforms.

Don't offer reimbursement for a problem until you're sure of all the facts, in addition to not mentioning it publicly.

Many properties are not aware that TripAdvisor and Yelp track IP addresses, so asking guests to write reviews while there is not a good idea as the reviews may get filtered out.

Reputation management is not just about online. It's about offline too. What are an inn's employees, former employees, and the associations and chambers that it may belong to saying? Are they recommending the business? Why or why not?

A business needs to monitor their online presence constantly. A negative story picked up by the news can snowball and put a property at serious risk of losing a substantial amount of business.

Steps for Responding to a Negative Review

- Remember to breathe deeply in between steps.
- Open your word processor and copy and paste the review into it.
- Read the review carefully, glean from it. Does the reviewer have a point that could have been fixed or avoided or is it something that can be fixed or avoided in the future?
- Deconstruct the review. Are there positive things in it? What are the negatives?
- Write the response (don't write the response right into the review site, even though some sites let one edit after the fact, the initial one usually gets e-mailed to the reviewer, so one is only playing catch-up to future readers) and make sure it's dated.
- Make sure the review gets read by others before it's posted, or at least wait a bit and reread it yourself before posting.
- If ever at a loss for how to respond, just apologize and let it go. The customer is always right in this case (even if they don't know what a medium rare steak is supposed to look like, or thinks a certain brand of shampoo is better than the one in the amenities basket). You aren't looking to change their mind and won't, so think beyond that. Acknowledgment is key.

References

www.phocuswright.com

Brian Payea, Head of Industry Relations; TripAdvisor; November 2015.

http://reknown.com

https://chefforfeng.wordpress.com

www.revinate.com

www.getfivestars.com/

.

CHAPTER 15

Online Travel Agents (OTAs)

In a recent talk at the University of Miami by Bob Diener, founder of Hotels.com, Bob shared with the audience why and how he started Hotels.com, what inspired his online baby turned giant, and how Hotels.com almost turned into a collection agency versus a viable online business. What struck me at this talk was Bob's ability to pivot, how he quickly realized that while profitable, large hotels had immense staff and healthy margins, their accounting departments were lacking and Hotels.com was paying the price. Collecting from these hotel properties was so difficult that Bob and his team decided to do something simple which changed the future of online hotel sales forever. Instead of going after the hotels to collect the commission fee owed to Hotels.com, the company reversed the payment process and began to collect all funds up front, in advance from the traveler, then turn around and paid the hotel once the reservation was satisfied.

Fast forward many years later and in comes Booking.com to the North American market with a novel idea, well actually, Bob's original payment model. Allow the hotel property to charge the guest directly and invoice the hotel for their commission owed after the stay. So, we digress, but not really. Bob's initial vision was simply too early. The lodging industry as a whole needed time to adapt to this idea of third parties selling their rooms online on their behalf. If not for the events of September 11 and the state of the economy, heavily discounted prices may not have been accepted by the hospitality community and this model might not be as popular as it has become, but so is life and it unfolds and we develop one step at a time.

In a strong economy with sufficient OTA providers for hotel properties to choose from, we're now nearing a time of balance. Room prices are leveling out, meaning OTAs are not dramatically lowering the cost of a property's rooms to attract customers, rather, diversity is the name of the game. Demand for something unique and different is taking precedent over the lowest price, as travelers want variety. Hence why not just hotels, but B&B's, Guesthouses, Yurts, Campgrounds, even hotel rooms in an Igloo or Underwater suites are popping up all over the globe. We are in a renaissance, a time for dramatic landscapes, individuality that is praised and sought out by travelers who want something unique and colorful for a night's experience. Consumers are more demanding: They want an experience and high quality service, not just a bed to lay their head, especially not a bed that looks like it has not been updated since the 1990s.

Rather an experience that justifies one's hard earned money and satisfies the need for adventure and fantasy. Airbnb is a perfect example of this; opening other peoples' homes to the world while connecting travelers to a local, personalized experience allows for a great deal of variety. Accommodations of all sorts have exploded, from funky buses turned into guestrooms, private Victorian apartments in San Francisco, homes in London with an English Garden (something that only the best of hotels provided previously), adobe stucco guest cottages in New Mexico with outdoor fireplaces and s'mores at night.

What does this mean for OTAs and independent lodging establishments? It means you, the individual property owner who at one point in time was told to standardize your rooms and make them fit into the norm of the hotel industry, are now encouraged to share your own personal style and service through mainstream travel portals unlike ever before. B&B and small boutique enthusiasts saw this value 30 years ago, enjoying this trend well before the millennials. Now we have the opportunity to share with the masses what's so unique and special about our independent properties. We can let our eclectic, artistic, and highly service oriented selves come out. Not to mention, we finally are able to partake in mainstream media at a price we can afford as commissions come closer and closer to the travel agent model of 10 percent per booking, a model that was accepted and liked by lodging establishments worldwide. We are not quite there yet, with 15 percent being the average OTA commission, but it's coming and these OTAs are now the preferred way to book. Nielsen reported that this year 52 percent of all U.S. lodging bookings will be facilitated by OTAs and that number keeps rising dramatically as travelers want faster results, all in one location, while they book with their smart phones using the credit card the OTA so conveniently stored for them.

Direct bookings at your establishment, especially on your website, is absolutely where innkeepers must focus much of their effort and time until the job is done, constantly monitoring and improving as nothing beats the customer coming to you direct. With that said, if a new establishment or struggling independent property wants an immediate uptick in sales, join as many OTAs as you can handle and see the bookings start to flow the minute you hit the final save button. In a trial with Hotels.com and a few dozen B&Bs I conducted in the early 2000s, I literally saw rooms booked 10 minutes after we hit the save button. Today activating properties takes a few days to a few weeks for the checks and balances process, but activation is still fast and it feels good to see an upswing in business so quickly, especially with no upfront cost to the property owner. Of course, time is a cost, but one well worth the return with OTAs.

As per a recent Cornell Hospitality study, researchers proved that something called the "Billboard or Halo Effect" is legit. OTAs allow your property to appear alongside the much larger brand names with multi-million dollar marketing budgets. Not only that, but the research also showed that every 10 percent of overall OTA business to your property generates another 10 percent in direct web bookings on your own website. Guests find your property on these OTA billboards and instead choose to seek you out directly, apart from the original billboard. Often the OTA is merely a vehicle for the consumer to become aware of your establishment.

When entering the world of OTAs, especially as a small lodging establishment that does not have a full-time marketing manager or front desk staff, it's imperative you think about your OTA plan of attack, keeping to a few well tried and traveled footsteps of independent lodging owners before you. Also, keep in mind that OTAs are more than just Hotels.com, Booking.com, and Expedia. Open your reach to Groupon which gobbles up your lucrative packages, TravelZoo, and others. I use the word OTA loosely to represent any online travel agent that sells my room nights either by themselves or packaged with another product.

Your OTA Plan of Attack

#1. Choose a Channel Manager

If your PMS (property management system) does not already connect to OTAs, then choose a Channel Manager that will do that for you. If your PMS charges an excessive commission for this service, on top of the average 15 percent an OTA charges, then consider an independent Channel Manager.

#2. Keep it Simple

While we are entering a renaissance whereby your unique charm, character, décor and service are desired, you must keep your offering organized and simple in such a way that it's easy to manage. How do you do that?

1. Standardize your rooms by bed size so that you can move a guest between rooms as long as the size matches their original choice. While you can and want to market your incredible rooms, do not promise anything too specific, other than room type and size if the customer books through the OTA. You must allow yourself to have flexibility to shift things around at the last minute or upgrade a guest when prudent to do so.
2. Categorize your room offerings in logical room types that people can understand. For example, a Standard, a Suite, and a Private Cottage.
3. Offer the same prices everywhere. If the rate is $200 a night on your website, then provide that same rate to OTAs. If the OTA offers at a discount it will be marginal as every dollar they discount is a dollar the OTA does not earn.
4. Same with packages. OTAs are beginning to incorporate your packages. Airbnb is taking this even further with local experiences that you can incorporate into your booking. Either way, stay consistent between your website and the OTA as managing separate packages and trying to remember what is offered where is difficult and will add more stress than is good for your health.

#3. Avoid Double Bookings

Double bookings are a small property's nightmare. While this can be a good problem to have for larger hotels as they have the capacity to shift guests around, smaller properties feel the squeeze. It's guaranteed someone will end up unhappy, so be careful. For example, a B&B owner in Mississippi offers 80 percent of his rooms to OTAs. Even if he's 100 percent empty, he only offers 80 percent allowing for last-minute issues, upgrades and direct bookings without worry. This particular innkeeper actually has an occupancy rate 10 percent higher than the average hotel because he's agile and smart, not to mention his property is stunning and by no means cookie-cutter. He makes his living on standing apart and being different, but behind the scenes he's mechanical in how he operates the marketing and sales of his property.

#4. Keep Your Cancellation Policy Attractive and Simple

Right off the bat I'm going to tell you that this is a major challenge for most small lodging owners. I see anywhere from three to six different cancellation policies at a given property covering a myriad of scenarios. OTAs will generally accommodate one or two cancellation policies and one or two payment terms. Again, keep things simple, it's easier for you in the end and trying to remember what cancellation you gave to which OTA, vs. a regular, consistent policy at the property can be exhausting. Keep it easy to manage and always find ways for the guests to win. Also, super strict cancellation policies, such as 30-day cancellation or no refund, are unattractive. The traveler is willing to accept a reasonable cancellation as they are intelligent and can understand the need for a property to protect themselves, but the days of planning vacations 30-days in advance is diminishing. OTAs have fully changed the landscape in which we live and millennials are booking same day. Per HospitalityNet:

> today's traveler will be the guy that is used to having all the information and services that he needs at the snap of a finger, a guy who is used to having options. He does not go out searching for services, the services and options must come to meet him. As a

result of this the travel industry will have to work even harder to satisfy him and his contemporaries.

Note: Your minimal length of stay and guarantee policies should be treated similarly to your cancellation policy. Stay consistent and as simple as possible. Even though running a property on your own is complicated, you will benefit from as many simple processes as possible. Whatever you do at your property, offer the same or even simpler to the OTAs you work with.

#5. Policies—Smoking, Pets, and Check-In

It is important to be crystal clear and to keep it simple when it comes to policies. You must communicate your rules effectively wherever you are listed or you will have problems with OTAs. Keep it black and white and avoid caveats and exceptions. In my experience, OTAs will hold you to your generic policy and will defend the guest first.

As most small properties do not have a 24-hour front desk or more than one or two people helping to check in guests, it's that much more important that you communicate to OTAs exactly how a guest checks in. Of course, you can't tell the public that the key's hidden under the door mat or the code to the lockbox to get the key, but there are ways to work around this and the OTAs understand the importance of this issue. Keyless entry is becoming increasingly popular.

Here are a few general tips to handle check-in:

1. *State your check-in policy in the description of your introductory text with any OTA and REPEAT.*
   While OTAs will of course have a section to note check-in hours, special instructions are tricky. If you're sensitive to this issue as most independent operators are, take special precaution to cover your bases as much as possible.
2. *Require all guests to contact you prior to arrival to best prepare for their stay.*
   This is not something you can enforce, meaning if a guest does not contact you prior to arrival there isn't really anything you can (or should) do, but you want to encourage as much communication

as possible. All OTAs will give you the guests' e-mail address after completing the booking, even if that e-mail address is masked it still arrives in the guests' inbox. Consider being proactive and e-mailing the guest your general check-in instructions as soon as you learn of the booking. It's super helpful and the guest cannot fault you for doing your best to communicate.

#6. Put Your Best Foot Forward with Great Photos

Despite the constant nagging and requests from OTAs and marketers, hotels and small lodging properties continue to produce mediocre photos of their properties that simply don't cut it for online sales. OTAs need high resolution, professional photos. Unless you have an upgraded smart phone, the best possible natural lighting and an immaculate room that is ready for shooting, professional photography pays for itself immediately. Your rooms will move much faster through OTAs with high-quality, professional photographs. As per the Center for Hospitality Research (CHR) at Cornell University, "when people are browsing through search results, they tend to look more frequently at hotel names than any other feature, and that pictures of the hotel appear to be hugely influential during both stages of the search." If you have an exceptional property with grand character, make sure to include extensive photos of public spaces, gardens, verandas, and food. Show experiences through photos such as breakfast in the garden, s'mores at night, an evening night cap, a roaring fireplace, a guest curled up in a corner reading a community book, and so on.

#7. Remote Properties: Check Your GPS and Driving Instructions

If your property is hard to get to or the Google GPS cannot find you, then make sure your driving instructions are listed with each OTA (written out in detail). Confusing arrivals are tough and start the guest out with a negative experience which is avoidable.

#8. Is Food Included?

If food is included in the room night, make sure you describe your food offering very clearly. I am not suggesting you set yourself up for extra work by guaranteeing a hot meal. In fact, I would avoid that if possible. Get descriptive in the text but use words like "you can expect this or something similar." Or "an expanded European breakfast buffet provided." Also, be very clear about dietary restrictions. People will assume you offer vegetarian and gluten-free options as other establishments are quickly making this a norm. If you can accommodate great, guests will love you for it. If you cannot, be specific. For example, your food description could read: "A delicious European breakfast buffet is included in your stay with various specialty breakfast dishes served each day such as blueberry stuffed French Toast or a savory Frittata. Please note, we may be able to accommodate food allergies but need at least 48 hours' notice to prepare for your dining experience, please contact the property directly to discuss your needs with one of our staff members who is standing by to ensure the best possible experience!"

#9. Make Sure You Get Paid

You would be surprised, or maybe not, by the number of small lodging owners who privately share with me that they often forget to collect on their OTA bookings. How is that possible you ask? Well, each OTA has their own unique payment process and they change often. One sends you the guest's credit card information and you must process the payment yourself at the time of checkout as well as any upfront guarantee payment previously specified. Another sends you a one-time use credit card which you process upon the guest's arrival. Yet another collects all the funds and then direct deposits to your bank account minus their fees. Others require you to charge the guest upon arrival and the OTA never collects the guest's credit card. My point is, this part can get complicated even if you have a great PMS (property management system), so stay on top of payments. Start by having a master list of each OTA you are working with and note how that particular OTA pays you and when. Set a day aside each month to analyze your OTA bookings and double check all bookings to ensure the reservation was completed and payment fulfilled. While this may be slightly tiresome to keep together, I'd rather count money coming in than going out!

Average Cost of Selling a Room Through OTAs

This varies from 10 to 15 percent, and although it sounds high, it's not really. According to TravelClick, it is estimated that independent hotels spent U.S. $8.50 to 12.50 per booking on their own website (i.e., to market the room and the costs associated with your website). Since there is no significant mass data made available to the public on the subject, these are expert assessments. This would be an equivalent of a 5 to 7 percent commission on the average hotel's own room price. Travel agencies have long charged similar fees.

It's not hard to see their value and the clear demand from travelers to search for lodging accommodations in as few central locations as possible with standardized search methods and stored credit cards. Considering that the lodging property does not pay for this service up front and only shells out a commission if the room is sold, I think this is a highly effective way to book business but must be done in such a way that the reward is worth the work and effort put in. The last thing anyone wants is any form of confusion or misunderstanding in your bookings of any form.

What's Next?

As OTAs make lodging and travel purchases easier and more inclusive, travelers are becoming more and more demanding. With quick access to information, peer reviews and a level playing field in regards to pricing, travelers are looking for more personalized service and a unique experience to choose their next getaway or even business trip. OTAs are gobbling up our once affordable pay-per-click advertising space now taking up the organic search placement and outbidding you for your primary keywords, often even your own property name! The two largest OTAs are booking over $50 billion in revenue per year and with recent acquisitions that number keeps climbing.

So, what's next? International travelers, especially those traveling from China, are on the rise and coming to the United States. Lucky for us small lodging establishments, in general these travelers seek out personalized accommodations. Accommodating yourself to communicate with this enormous travel segment is going to be your greatest challenge, but is not impossible. Additionally, you must work with your merchant provider to accept the Chinese pin system which is slightly different from the United States and will deter online bookings if not updated.

Additionally, if you are looking to expand to a few vacation rentals as you have your nightly business down to a science and want to expand, the vacation rental market is booming and you certainly can benefit. Site's like VRBO and Airbnb cater to this market, as does HomeAway.

On the service side, not only are technology advances enhancing the guests' experience inside your rooms, but the service you provide can actually be outsourced! Companies catering primarily to the hosts of Airbnb have popped up to facilitate personal check-ins. This may be the part of the business that you hold back for your own personal touch, but options are out there and helping independent lodging owners that cannot juggle it all. Call centers are available to answer your phone when you cannot grab it, posing as an experienced staff member who can answer the top 10 to 20 questions that are routinely asked over and over. The guest then provides their credit card and the phone representative fills out the reservation information for the guest. I have called a few B&B establishments myself and had absolutely no idea I was talking to anyone but the innkeeper as the phone operator was friendly, knowledgeable and encouraged the booking. I was amazed when I found out.

And then there are the millennials. A population larger than the baby boomers, this energetic generation seeks adventure, experience and travel. This is the most plugged in, peer oriented generation in history and our perfect customer. They want unique, memorable and personal experiences, which is exactly what the small lodging owner is suited to provide.

A renaissance is upon us, a time when being unique and highly personal is desirable, so enjoy this cycle and ride the OTA's wave to profitability.

Takeaways

- Need more occupancy fast? OTAs may be the way to go.
- Pay attention to the fine print of payment methods and follow up to make sure your hard work is compensated.

- Be very specific and avoid gray areas, especially in check-in procedures, rules and limitations you impose, and menu availability.

Resources

Examples of Channel Managers for Independent Lodging Establishments:
Myallocator (www.cloudbeds.com/myallocator/)
TravelClick (www.travelclick.com/en/product-services/reservations-solutions/
  channel-management)
SiteMinder (www.siteminder.com/channel-manager/)
Google Instructions on adding your Business to their Map Locator:
https://support.google.com/business/answer/6174435?hl=en
Millennials and Lodging
www.nytimes.com/2016/04/10/travel/millennials-hotels.html

References

Bob Diener: www.linkedin.com/in/bobdiener
Siteminder (Nielson): www.siteminder.com/r/trends-advice/hotel-insights/fast-
  forward-to-2017-what-will-the-global-hotel-industry-look-like/
Cornell: http://scholarship.sha.cornell.edu/chrpubs/2/
http://blog.ecornell.com/the-billboard-effect/
https://sha.cornell.edu/centers-institutes/chr/about/news/press/prdetails.
  html?id=1026
Hospitality.net: www.hospitalitynet.org/news/4080188.html
TravelClick: www.travelclick.com/en/news-events/in-the-news/hospitality-net-
  %E2%80%93-hotel-adr-rise-vs-distribution-channels-cost-what-hoteliers-
  need-calculate
Priceline Annual Report: http://files.shareholder.com/downloads/PCLN/383789
  0179x0xS1075531-16-84/1075531/filing.pdf
Expedia Annual Report: http://files.shareholder.com/downloads/EXPE/149169
  2058x0x874391/ED44C98A-C0BB-4FC7-BDF9-19C7C2347F34/EXPE_
  Q4_2015_Earnings_Release_FINAL.pdf

APPENDIX

Five-Month Detailed Marketing Plan

Online Marketing and Distribution Proposal

Executive Summary

Over the past 5 years, there have been seismic shifts in how consumers research and purchase lodging. The proliferation of review sites, social media marketing, and online distribution of inventory have left hoteliers unprepared and losing opportunities. Many see their revenues dropping as they struggle to market effectively with new online technologies, primarily because they are "off the grid." This formal marketing plan serves as a blueprint for any innkeepers curious as to how a resort outlines their marketing initiatives.

Getting Your Engines Revving and Rooms Selling

The role of this plan is to create an outline with a multiphased beginning and proposed roll out with key performance indicators throughout (see the following), along with a timeline to support the smooth and timely delivery of this plan.

Phase One: Month 1

Define the Brand

It is essential that the property have a clearly defined brand from which all marketing efforts will flow. Working one-on-one with a management team helps brainstorm and narrow down the key ingredients or components that will establish the property as a unique, exclusive getaway with an action plan to communicate this new luxury property to the tourism industry and traveling public. A comprehensive marketing plan will follow the "8 Ps" of your luxury brand (product, place and time, price, promotion, process, physical environment, people, productivity and quality).

Figuring out how to position the brand, who the target demographics are, price points, what services will be launched in the near future, and how the team intends to expand in the months to come are the main objectives in this first month.

Phase Two: Months 2 and 3

Create an Online Marketing Strategy

Steps to ensure on-time execution and quality, including:

- **Bookable Website** Focused on the guest experience, not the vacation rental owner. Create the editorial for the website as well as the graphic and video direction. Monitor progress with improvement strategies.
- **Usability** Ensure maximum ease of use and navigation on the website to ensure high booking conversion.
- **Google Analytics Set** Monitor top referring sources and ongoing, developing demographics on travelers who have visited the new site.
- **Search Engine Optimization (SEO)** On-site analysis and recommendations, monitoring top referring sources, link building opportunities and recommendations, analysis of local placement with improvement strategies.
- **Pay-Per-Click Management (PPC)** Management of Google Adwords and MSN Adcenter (Bing and Yahoo) Accounts with time-sensitive updates of all specials and packages to promote current offerings.
- **Google Analytics and ROI Analysis** Revenue tracking integrated with the inn's reservation system to can tell you exactly how much money is made on every link to the website.

- **Reputation Management** Monitoring your presence on Trip Advisor, Yelp, Google Local, YouTube, and other pertinent online sources (including Roatan sources).
- **Social Media Consulting** Social media set up and ongoing monitoring and consultation
- **e-Newsletter Communications** Set up a constant contact or MailChimp account with two to four templates for guests, travel agents and the local population.
- **Online Graphics and Special Offers** Create online special offers and graphics to drive opt-in subscribers to newsletter.

Phase Three: Months 4 and 5

All Engines Started

- Release fully functional and approved first-generation website, begin direct website bookings (after BETA site has been tested and approved).
- Drop travel industry press release to travel editors.
- Contract and connect with distribution networks such as Hotels.com, Booking.com, TravelZoo, and more.
- Set up the consortia and corporate RFP contracting for group bookings.
- Unleash opt-in campaign for monthly e-newsletter focused on the traveler.

Nonessentials (Though Quickly Becoming Essential)

- **Video:** Compile two to three videos from approved images with music overlaid until more information is collected on the client demographics or a budget is allocated for streaming video.
- **Mobile Marketing:** Create a mobile friendly version of the website including integrated SEO development, unique messaging, special promotions, and monitoring.

- **Blogging:** Starting out monthly, moving to weekly blog highlighting what makes your inn different or unique (essential for search engine optimization).

Key Performance Indicators

- Brand statement
- Website launch
- Website optimized
- Distribution channels opened.
- Rooms begin to sell through website and distribution channels
- Social media and reputation monitoring up and running, process in place for regular contribution and monitoring
- PPC and monitoring in place to evaluate ROI for online advertisement
- Blog launched with first four articles posted

This marketing plan was originally written by Marie Lanier for a small upscale Caribbean resort.

Bass and Baskets:
An Innkeeper's Passions

Who knew a simple trip weekend could be so fateful? It started when Ed and Debbie Franko took an excursion to Ohio's Longaberger basketry center, staying overnight at their very first bed and breakfast. "We liked it so much that we thought this was something we could do someday when we retired," said Debbie.

On their way home to St. Louis, the pair daydreamed about opening their own inn, cleverly devising a name for their bed-and-breakfast-to-be that reflected their passions and even imagining a sign made: "Bass & Baskets, est. 1998."

They returned to their regular lives. Debbie to teaching elementary school kids and Ed to managing fast-food restaurants. But the seed was planted in each of their minds, and the dream refused to fade. Soon the couple toured lakefront properties with a realtor, focusing on the Lake of the Ozarks, where Ed had participated in many bass-fishing tournaments.

One Sunday morning Debbie and Ed drove past the home of an old fishing buddy and happened to notice a "For Sale, No Realtors" sign in the yard next door. Punching in the phone number, Ed realized he was calling someone who lived in his old hometown of Granite City, IL "I think it was meant to be," he said. After just a day of negotiations, they walked away with the key.

All that remained was to quit their jobs, sell their home, remodel the 1960s cottage and start a business that neither of them knew anything about. "I guess you might call us daring people," commented the gregarious Ed.

"Our friends thought we were crazy," added Debbie, "because we were leaving good jobs and a beautiful home to move to a rundown place with no money." Drawing on a strong, shared vision based on their passion they opened their doors in October 2001. In the midst of the travel downturn, the Frankos knew they had to do something special to ensure the occupancy they needed. Like all entrepreneurs, they prepared the basics and made sure their website and other marketing materials were in good order—but they needed more oomph. True to their business name and their respective passions, the couple would offer guests "Bass & Baskets."

Debbie, who had a strong appreciation for handicrafts, shared the beautiful, handcrafted Longaberger baskets for sale at the inn and generously incorporated them into the decor, in the spirit of bounty, she filled them with homemade goods such as delectable zucchini bread.

Furthermore, in the Frankos' spacious main drawing room, Deb began offering quilting bees, scrapbooking parties, and couples cooking. In preparation, she secured plenty of layout space and outlets to plug in necessary equipment. She marketed the classes through the scrapbook supply dealer and through her ongoing postings on hobby sites.

Meanwhile, Ed was a champion fisherman. The very cove where they lived was marked "good fishing" and played a big part in their decision to buy the property. Even now, the Frankos own and operate a fully licensed guide service too—Big Ed's Guide Service to take advantage of the fantastic bass-fishing available on the lake. Ed also considered offering high-end specialty fishing gear to guests, which would create another profit center.

One focus of the Bass & Baskets specialty guest packages involved the fantastic shopping at the Osage Beach Shopping Mali, where Debbie takes guests on shopping excursions. But the onsite sales at the inn became equally enticing. Debbie sold Private Quarter linens, which are on all the inn's beds so that guests experience them firsthand.

Ed and Debbie Franko managed to meld their interests with a good marketing plan so that business and pleasure will always be enjoyable—and lucrative, too, as the inn has maintained operation for more than 15 years.

Putting Heads in Country Beds

Rural and heritage travel focused marketing. This information comes from live, in-person presentations and audience feedback at independent lodging conferences from Canada to Florida.

Trends That Favor the Independent Hospitality Industry in North America

Short vacations Shorter holidays tend to favor the lodging industry. People are taking ever-shorter trips in North America, often a driving trip, often a getaway that's 3 or 4 hours drive away.

Millennials seek out experiences to add to their perspective and the chance to stay as a local appeals to them more than the tried-and-true certainty of a hotel.

Baby Boomers taking their families traveling Boomers are taking their children and grandchildren on the road to show them this wonderful country. Some places are set up ideally to host families a family room is really helpful and a great attraction for families.

Golden Agers active retirees Golden guests are really fueling independent prosperity, traveling happily while they still have the time and health. They are easy guests, stay longer, and fuel the local economy by buying gifts for family and friends.

Sophistication Many people travel the world, creating an experienced, sophisticated traveler base.

Example Initiatives That Actually Worked in Manitoba!

EQ Check out Destination Canada's Explorer Quotient at http://en. destinationcanada.com/resources-industry/explorer-quotient

B&B MB brochure B&B MB has a great small booklet: 5,000 copies, printed annually, widely distributed. "Because people still read. And people like to read while they're traveling and they pick things up."

Innovative publicity *The Cinnamon Bun Trail In search of sweet treats across rural Manitoba* produced jointly by five Manitoba Tourism Associations (Parkland, North, Interlake, Eastern, Central Plains) with Travel Manitoba. A great idea! See it at http://admin.getawaysinmanitoba.ca/ FileUpload/region1/files/cinnamon_bun_trails_2012_brochure.pdf

Signage Evergreen Gate's "official highway sign" cost $1,000 upfront, which is a lot, but is maintained by the Province. B&Bs should look into this. European visitors like to make a last-minute choice and just get off the road when they see a sign.

Inclusiveness Complements to the B&B conference organizers for providing sign language translations for participants at a conference. Inclusiveness is a social imperative of Manitoba hospitality, and the one that guests greatly appreciate.

APPENDIX 2

List of Possible Marketing Initiatives

These are specific examples, based on activities, natural features, and affinity groups.

The following is a compilation of the results from Montana Lodging and Hospitality Association meeting in Butte, Montana, which consisted first of a morning session titled, "Stakeholders in a Destination: Increasing Visitors through Collaborative Efforts," which was an informative overview of how to involve all stakeholders in an area to derive a cohesive plan to drive tourism to that area followed by an afternoon interactive roundtable discussion. It is organized in three target marketing categories: National Parks Heritage and History, Outdoors, and Romantic Getaways and Lifestyle.

National Parks Heritage and History

National Parks Target Markets:

- Office of Tourism
- Bus tours
- Driving tours
- Families
- International travelers
- Niche: snowmobiling, hiking, bird watching, and so on
- Outdoor clubs: photography clubs, bicycling, canoeing, and so on
- Universities, school field trips
- Seniors, RV travelers, campers
- AAA, AARP, Canadian Auto Association
- Elder Hostel, day trips, 1 to 5 days

What people are looking for

- Landmarks
- Wildlife
- History
- Geology
- Driving tours

Internet

- What to do
- Geography
- Accommodations
- Travel about
- Route or directions from airport
- Podcast or regularly updated news feed

Plan

- Research what the park has to offer, location

Heritage and History Ideas

- International Travelers Asia, Canada, or Europe
- Own family history
- Farm exploration
- Dude ranch or working ranch
- Mining or Gold Rush
- Westward Trail and Pioneer Settlements
- Waterways
- Preserved areas specific sites
- Indian Reservations
- Ghost Towns
- Archaeology or Geology
- Museums
- Battlefields or forts

Getting the Word Out: Outdoors

Hunting, Fishing, Skiing, Hot Springs, Hiking, Biking, Water Sports, and so on

- Packages
- Partnering with outfitters and guides
- Information to distribute at a county level
- Partner with the state to market your area
- Use social media sites, create links to your presence on Facebook, Twitter, LinkedIn, Instagram, and so on and make sure each of those links is featured on each social media site (e.g., have links to your Twitter and LinkedIn page on your Facebook page) (Target specific groups): Advertise specials
- PayPerClick advertising
- Clubs in other regions
- PR and family trips
- FourSquare, smartphone apps, and so on
- Educate community
- Share ideas for events with your local Tourism Bureau, Chamber of Commerce and Convention and Visitors Bureau (CVB)
- Incentives for referrals from guides or outfitters
- Shuttles to or from outdoor activities
- Local events or activities tickets available at front desk
- Packages thinking outside the box
- Utilize school programs

Romantic Getaways and Lifestyle

#1 Feeders in state WA, OR, MN, ID, ND, SD, Canada

Targets

- Weekend getaways
- Culinary travel and cooking demos

- Festivals
- Theater
- Anniversaries, reunions, receptions guest list
- February plan date
- Shopping meccas
- Hot springs and beauty spots
- Amtrak stopovers
- Brunch, Dinner, Wine trains, or Cruise

Forecasting and Liaising

- Newspaper lifestyle
- VIA
- Sunset
- Canadian papers
- Regional travel guides

Example Specials or Packages

- Please your Honey Button: Her interest is premiere
- Spa Weekend for Two... + Golf
- Yellowstone Snowmobile Motel Packages
- Sporting events
- Hot Springs Weekend Getaways
- Girlfriend Getaways Spa, shopping, fine dining, champagne tasting, and so on
- Crafts Weekend: scrapbooking, quilting, knitting
- Harley Clubs
- Car Clubs

APPENDIX 3

Top Tips from Successful Properties

In the course of speaking and teaching at over a hundred small lodging conferences there emerged a handful of ideas that are tried-and-true and have led to standout success for those properties which have implemented them.

Calendar—First and foremost, creating a comprehensive marketing calendar at least 6 months in advance which will be your guiding star for the months ahead (start at any month and add to the calendar monthly or bimonthly).

This calendar will encompass the drafts and documents you create for marketing such as your newsletter, returning guest special offers, blogs, and social media posts. It will be informed by annual public holidays and celebrations which are always easy to build specials and buzz around like Valentine's Day, Memorial weekend, and so on. It will also include the intelligence you have collected on community events, local college, and other educational events and dates, including art shows and musical performances, sporting events, and any other date for a happening which is established and to which perspective guests might travel. Of course, the holidays and special events should all be incorporated into your newsletter and social media to give folks a reason to follow you. Your comprehensive calendar will help you sleep at night knowing that you have your marketing bases covered so you don't have any nights where you sit bolt upright in bed because of a suddenly remembered fair, event, or holiday that had slipped your mind. Even better when you have zero inspiration or energy just a glance at the calendar will give you plenty to do!

(Refer to the chapters Total Media Marketing, Marketing Your Passions, and Managing Your Social Reputation for more info and ideas.)

Make your website a hub—By making your website a one stop shop for a trip to your area—featuring surrounding attractions and adventures—a potential guest realizes they don't need to book multiple lodgings for a several night trip. They can simply stay with you for their whole stay and drive to the other places as a fun day trip. Most folks know that "stay and play" is way more relaxing than packing and unpacking daily and if you make it crystal clear with mini maps and concise directions of times involved you can sell your guest easily on the benefits of staying multiple nights with you. Remember that multiple night stays are more profitable than any other due to economies of scale, savings on housekeeping and laundry, but most of all the opportunity to turn a guest into a longtime friend and fan.

Viral marketing—The single best tip I ever heard on this topic was from an innkeeper in a lovely but rural part of Michigan, 3 hours from any major metro area, who managed to maintain very good occupancy. When asked about their tips for achieving those rates, going beyond the usual winning strategies of hospitality, great breakfasts, beautiful décor and up-to speed facilities and amenities, the husband finally admitted "well then we have our sign." When I arrived at the lodge I had noted a striking, large and hand carved sign on the front lawn right at the bottom of the entry stairs. So here is the trick: This sign is sized and painted so that the name of the inn and its town and state are unmistakable and all placed so that a couple standing in front of the sign is beautifully framed but the inn's name and so on are still visible. Our industrious innkeeper simply asked each guest as they arrived or departed (based on management's time availability) if he might take a picture of them before the sign and if he could then send them the image. Be sure to ask for privacy reasons. But 90 percent of guests were happy to agree and when they received their image via e-mail upon their return home you can believe that it went viral on all of their social media and to all their friends, all without the need to mention the place where the happy holiday took place: It's right there on the image.

The generous innkeeper—Create your own "inn currency" with a catchy color and graphics and denominate in $25 to $50 "bills" (dependent on the price of your locale) and hand them out lavishly. For example, every property soon gets tapped and sometimes tapped out for free night stays to be used for local fund raising events, so imagine the impact of saying "oh, you are expecting 100 folks to attend that dinner? Terrific, we'll donate $5,000 to the effort in the form of a "$50 off your first night" certificate which you can add to each place setting!" From that you get a happy community organizer and the reputation of a prosperous and generous innkeeper spreading all over the community. Be sure to print up plenty of your "currency" and hand out to one and all, make your place the first your neighbors and fellow citizens think of when they need an extra room for a guest (after all, they already have the voucher)!

Be consistent—Finally, my favorite for getting motivated when marketing is the last thing on your mind or mood. Simply do something every day to move your occupancy upward. Some days it may be a big effort like the writing, batching, and sending of a monthly communiqué. Other days may take a more low key approach and you simply mosey around town with a stack of your currency and say "Hi" to fellow business people, and leave a few of your "$50 off your first night" bills. Don't forget the barber and hair stylist, manicure places and gym, target places where folks feel relaxed and receptive!

Feeling more creative than constructive? Whip up your new strawberry signature scones. Photograph a plate of them looking picture perfect then post to all your usual spots including, of course, your website where season specific images and recipes can be rotated in and out to serve you well for a long time. The creative urge might lead you to make a new seasonal door wreath or table arrangement this works too. You can never have too many fresh and focused images to represent your place in the media.

If it's snowing or raining cats and dogs stay in and phone your contact at the college or community center or church and see if there are some newly scheduled activities which will bring potential guests to your area. Offer some inn discount currency and then just pop in the mail and add the date of the event to your ever-expanding calendar. Sip your coffee and congratulate yourself on yet another day you have done your daily marketing chore.

Author Biographies

Pamela Lanier

Founder and Director | EcoGo.org; Consultant

www.pamelalanier.com

Pamelalanier@yahoo.com

Pamela Lanier is the author of 20 travel titles in over 130 editions. She is the founder of Bed & Breakfasts, Inns, and Guest Houses International and established the TravelGuides.com network. Pamela has increased her involvement in ecotourism and sustainable travel, leading presentations at the World Conservation Congress in Jeju, South Korea and the World Wilderness Congress in Salamanca, Spain. World Travel Market, London, and World Parks Congress, Sydney, among 130 conference presentations worldwide.

Marie Lanier

Founder and CEO | BBConnect

www.MarieLanier.com

info@marielanier.com

B&B thought leader with over 20 years of hands on experience raising the bar on behalf of the small lodging and B&B industry. Marie has led thousands of small properties into the mainstream and was the first woman to bring B&B's to Hotels.com followed by many more online travel agencies. Marie continues to champion on behalf of the well-being of the independent lodging owner.

List of Contributors

Marci Bracco Cain
Chapter: Mastering Public Relations
Owner, Managing Partner | Chatterbox Public Relations
www.chatterboxpr.com
marci@chatterboxpublicrelations.com

Julia Guerra
Chapter: Your Social Media Presence
Director of Operations | The International Ecotourism Society (TIES)
www.juliaguerra.com
digitalmarketing@juliaguerra.com

TIES is a nonprofit organization dedicated to promoting sustainable tourism practices around the world. Julia specializes in social media marketing, tourism branding, and webinars, and, through her work at TIES, she works and instructs ecolodges, tour operators, and destinations on how to leverage their digital marketing campaigns. Julia is passionate about scuba diving, hiking, and anything sustainable tourism related.

Lisa Kolb
Chapter: SEO (Search Engine Optimization)
President and Co-Founder | Acorn Internet Services, Inc.
www.acorn-is.com
877-226-7699

Together Lisa and her husband Mark have over 40 years of combined experience that can be put to work for you. In 1996, after almost a decade of solely working in the corporate world of software development and design, they moved to Colorado Springs to open a bed and breakfast. While doing software support and development for their bed and breakfast and a local bed and breakfast organization's website, the need for a low-cost quality solution for the online marketing needs of other small businesses became glaringly apparent.

Dr. Carolin Lusby

Chapter: Demographics Make a Difference
Assistant Professor, PhD | Chaplin School of Hospitality and Tourism Management
clusby@fiu.edu

Carolin is an assistant professor at FIU and believes in the power of travel to transform lives and create sustainable livelihoods. Besides teaching and research, she leads regular trips and is the CEO of a small tourism nonprofit.

Patricia McCauley

Chapter: Website Fundamentals for Innkeepers
President | InsideOut Solutions
www.insideout.com
pat@insideout.com
(360) 683-5774 ext 302

Patricia has presented at numerous conferences across North America and is available to speak on current marketing and web trends in the tourism industry.

Heather Turner

Chapter: The Rating Game: Leveraging Consumer Reviews
Chief | Forfeng Designs
www.chefforfeng.wordpress.com
heather@forfengdesigns.com | forfengdesigns@gmail.com

Heather Turner aka Forfeng is a graduate of the Culinary Institute of America and has spent over 20 years in the restaurant business. She trained under one of the PBS Series "Great Chefs of America," Chef Yves Labbe at four star acclaimed restaurant, Le Cheval D'or and has been the Executive Chef at Bellini's Restaurant, The Cliff House at Stowe

Mt. Resort and Harvest Market in Northern Vermont and at The Olde Inn on Cape Cod.

Kris Ullmer

Chapter: Working with Associations and Travel Agents (Associations portion)
Executive Director | Professional Association Innkeepers International
www.paii.org
paii@paii.org
715-257-0128

From Innkeeper to Wisconsin B&B Association Executive Director to PAII, Kris shares her passion for innkeeping with travelers, educates innkeepers on trends and best practices, and advocates for equitable regulations for the industry. Founded in 1987, PAII is the nation's largest innkeeping association, and the strategic partnership with the American Hotel and Lodging Association (AH&LA) further amplifies recognition of small, independently owned inns and Bed & Breakfasts. In 2003 she started her own business which combines hospitality consulting with marketing for a variety of businesses.

Erika A. Richter

Chapter: Working with Associations and Travel Agents (Travel Agents Portion)
Director of Communications | American Society of Travel Agents
www.ASTA.org
erichter@asta.org
(W) 703.739.6806

Toni Lanotte-Day

Chapter: Working with Associations and Travel Agents (Travel Agents Portion)
Toni Tours, Inc.
www.tonitours.net
toni@tonitours.net
W. 516-369-5738

Julia P. Douglas

Chapter: Working with Associations and Travel Agents (Travel Agents Portion)

JETSET World Travel, Inc.

www.jetsetworldtravel.com

312.574.1181 (office/fax)

Kelly Bergin

Chapter: Working with Associations and Travel Agents (Travel Agents Portion)

OASIS | Palm Coast Travel

www.OASISAgent.com

800.613.8380 ext. 5120

Christopher (Chris) J. Dane

Chapter: Working with Associations and Travel Agents (Travel Agents Portion)

President | Hickory Global Partners

www.HickoryTravel.com

CDane@HickoryTravel.com

phone: +1 561.900.2535 ext 2050

Matthew D. Upchurch

Chapter: Working with Associations and Travel Agents (Travel Agents Portion)

CEO | Virtuoso®

www.virtuoso.com | blog.virtuoso.com

Tel: 212-588-8232

Index

OTHER TITLES IN OUR TOURISM AND HOSPITALITY MANAGEMENT COLLECTION

Betsy Bender Stringam, New Mexico State University, Editor

- *The Good Company: Sustainability in Hospitality, Tourism, and Wine* by Robert H. Girling, Pamela Lanier, and Heather Dawn Gordy
- *Coastal Tourism, Sustainability, and Climate Change in the Caribbean: Beaches and Hotels, Volume I* by Martha Honey, Kreg Ettenger, and Samantha Hogenson
- *Coastal Tourism, Sustainability, and Climate Change in the Caribbean: Supporting Activities, Volume II* by Martha Honey, Kreg Ettenger, and Samantha Hogenson

Announcing the Business Expert Press Digital Library

Concise e-books business students need for classroom and research

This book can also be purchased in an e-book collection by your library as

- a one-time purchase,
- that is owned forever,
- allows for simultaneous readers,
- has no restrictions on printing, and
- can be downloaded as PDFs from within the library community.

Our digital library collections are a great solution to beat the rising cost of textbooks. E-books can be loaded into their course management systems or onto students' e-book readers.
The **Business Expert Press** digital libraries are very affordable, with no obligation to buy in future years. For more information, please visit **www.businessexpertpress.com/librarians**. To set up a trial in the United States, please email **sales@businessexpertpress.com**.

www.ingramcontent.com/pod-product-compliance
Lightning Source LLC
Chambersburg PA
CBHW050106210326
41519CB00015BA/3846

9 7 8 1 6 3 1 5 7 5 9 6 9